Innovative Approaches, Practices, and Strategies in Adult Education

VOICES FROM THE FIELD

The state of adult education is in a unique position. There are numerous adults who are fully aware that by obtaining an education it could provide them with better skills and better earning potential, but they are also aware that they may not be academically prepared to handle the rigor that is required to accomplish earning the college credits necessary for obtaining a degree or a certificate. Many adults yearn for a college degree, yet do not have the blueprint to be successful in this arena.

—*Dr. Naesea S. Price*, **Professor of Developmental English and Reading**

The state of adult education today is at a transformative crossroads, characterized by a heightened focus on accessibility, inclusivity, and technology-driven solutions. With the rise of online learning platforms and the integration of personalized learning paths, adult education has evolved to meet learners where they are, both geographically and in their learning journeys. There's an increasing emphasis on skills-based training and competency development that aligns with the rapidly changing job market, making education more relevant and applicable to real-world needs. However, challenges remain, particularly in bridging the digital divide and ensuring equitable access to quality education for all adults, regardless of their socioeconomic status or background. The future of adult education lies in its ability to adapt, innovate, and embrace a learner-centered approach that empowers individuals to achieve their personal and professional goals.

—*Dr. Reginald Stroble*, **Director of Student Success**

We as educators are adapting to meet the needs of our adult learners; we no longer build our schedules and platforms to fit our institutional history. Students and technology have forced even the most reticent institutions to rethink how we meet the needs of the populations we serve. Platforms that respond to the needs and expectations of the learners, remote synchronous, asynchronous, synchronous nights or weekends, and accelerated terms are readily available. We are allowing students to explore, use AI, and understand the implications, advantages, and pitfalls, which are all part of the evolution of education.

—*Susan Delker-Grauel*, **Associate Professor and Department Chair of Academic Development**

As the workplace continues to evolve and as more people embrace the benefits of lifelong learning as both a career and a wellness pursuit, it is critical to understand the unique needs of adults in the educational environment.

Now more than ever, we need instructional strategies and educational practices that address the unique needs of the adult learner. It is time to have a forum to share the exceptional work being done by colleagues who are embracing andragogical approaches and to create a call to action to support the needs of this growing population of learners.

—Marcia Dawson, **Associate Professor of English**

Research, Theory, and Practice Within Academic Affairs

Series Editors
Antione D. Tomlin and Sherella Cupid

The mission of the Research, Theory, and Practice Within Academic Affairs series seeks to explore current trends, practices, and challenges within academic affairs. This book series will include a plethora of topics with particular attention to the personal and live experiences of individuals who work in higher education academic affairs spaces in various colleges and universities. The intended audience is academic affairs administrators, leaders, educators, policymakers, researchers, and others interested in learning more about the experiences of academic affairs professionals.

OTHER TITLES IN THE SERIES

Escape the Cape, From Existing to Evolving: Amplifying Voices of Black and Brown Women in the Mental Health Profession

Faculty Success in the Academy: Tips, Tools, and Resources for Success

It is More Than the Miracle Question: Deconstructing Solution Focused Therapy

Innovative Approaches, Practices, and Strategies in Adult Education

Edited by

Antione D. Tomlin
Anne Arundel Community College, USA

United Kingdom – North America – Japan
India – Malaysia – China

Emerald Publishing Limited
Emerald Publishing, Floor 5, Northspring, 21-23 Wellington Street, Leeds LS1 4DL

First edition 2026

Copyright © 2026 by Emerald Publishing Limited.
All rights of reproduction in any form reserved.

Cover photo: iStock and DrAfter123

Reprints and permissions service
Contact: www.copyright.com

No part of this book may be reproduced, stored in a retrieval system, transmitted in any form or by any means electronic, mechanical, photocopying, recording or otherwise without either the prior written permission of the publisher or a licence permitting restricted copying issued in the UK by The Copyright Licensing Agency and in the USA by The Copyright Clearance Center. Any opinions expressed in the chapters are those of the authors. Whilst Emerald makes every effort to ensure the quality and accuracy of its content, Emerald makes no representation implied or otherwise, as to the chapters' suitability and application and disclaims any warranties, express or implied, to their use.

British Library Cataloguing in Publication Data
A catalogue record for this book is available from the British Library

ISBN: 978-1-80592-294-0 (Print hardback)
ISBN: 978-1-80592-296-4 (Print paperback)
ISBN: 978-1-80592-293-3 (Ebook)
ISBN: 978-1-80592-295-7 (EPUB)

Typeset by TNQ Tech
Cover design by TNQ Tech

TABLE OF CONTENTS

About the Editor ix

About the Contributors xi

Introduction xvii

SECTION 1
REDEFINING SUCCESS THROUGH MULTIPLE MEASURES ASSESSMENTS

1 Adult Learner Success in Community Colleges: Improving Outcomes Using Multiple Measures Assessments 3
   Johnathon E. Paape

2 Transforming Pedagogy and Empowering Faculty: The Impact of a Center for Teaching Excellence on Adult Education 15
   Stacy Ybarra Evans

3 Empowering Adult Learners Through Case-Based Instruction: A New Approach to Employability Skills 23
   Alexis Guethler and Sharon Ultsch

SECTION 2

SUPPORTING DIVERSE LEARNERS AND PEDAGOGICAL INNOVATION

4 First-Gen, Second Chance: Identifying and Supporting First-Gen Adult Learners 39
   La'Tonya "LT" Rease Miles

5 Unlocking Authentic D.E.I.B. Leadership in Adult Education: Leveraging 3 Keys of Emotional Intelligence in the Workplace 49
   Airies Davis

6 Creativity as a Docking Station for a Freer Future: Creative Dispatches + Radical Re-Imaginings From Black Doctoral Students 69
   Gretchen Rudham, Jacqueline Hayden and Rosalind Fleming

SECTION 3

FLEXIBILITY AND ADAPTABILITY IN HIGHER EDUCATION

7 Internationalization of Higher Education: International Students' Perspectives 93
   Merab Mushfiq

8 Driving Change in Higher Education: Strategies for Implementing Successful Organizational Transformation 103
   Jennifer Holland

9 Andragogy in Online Education: Empowering Adult Learners 115
   Marcedes Butler

10 Promoting Flexibility as a Means of Success for Adult Learners 127
   Joyvina Evans

ABOUT THE EDITOR

Antione D. Tomlin, PhD: Rooted in core values like Autonomy, Flexibility, Learning, Respect, Transparency, Honesty, and Fun, I live and breathe principles that not only shape my life but also guide my interactions with others. As a proud native of Baltimore City, these values have been my compass in navigating life's journey. Being a first-generation undergrad and grad student, I recognize the transformative power of education, a value intricately tied to my passion for continuous learning. This passion steered me into a fulfilling career in higher education, where I've been teaching English since 2013. The classroom, for me, is an ever-inspiring space filled with dedicated students who continually fuel my curiosity and growth. Beyond teaching, I wear the hat of a trained and certified Life and Engagement Coach, proudly holding the Professional Certified Coach (PCC) credential from the International Coach Federation (ICF). Feel free to explore more about my coaching venture, Best AT Coaching!, LLC. As a Baltimore native, I earned my academic stripes from local institutions: a BS in psychology from Stevenson University, an MA in higher education administration and student affairs from Morgan State University, and a PhD in language, literacy, and culture from the University of Maryland, Baltimore County. My current research focuses on the experiences of Black and Brown faculty, staff, and students in higher education.

ABOUT THE CONTRIBUTORS

Marcedes Butler, also known as Dr Sadie, is a dedicated educational leader and scholar with extensive experience in academic advising and adult education. As a Research Associate, BGCSNV Fellow, and faculty member at UNLV's College of Education, she specializes in Research Methods and First-Year Seminar courses. Dr Butler is also the founder of AcademicHelp101.com, an educational consulting firm focused on fostering academic success. She holds a Doctorate in Educational Psychology from USC and a Master's in Counseling, SDHE from CSULB.

Airies Davis, a practitioner-scholar with over 15 years of experience, leads strategic teams focused on diversity, equity, inclusion, and belonging. As the Founder and Chief Strategist of etiKID Academy LLC, a certified Minority and Women-owned small business dedicated to etiquette education, she is deeply committed to social justice and change. Dr Davis has contributed to organizations such as BetterUp, Deloitte, Chicago Public Schools, Monster Worldwide, and Merrill Lynch Capital. She serves as the inaugural Director of Workforce Development and Adjunct Faculty at Dominican University, a Hispanic Serving Institution, where she teaches undergraduate business and PhD level social justice and entrepreneurship courses. Her research-driven initiatives advance workforce development and global economic resilience. Dr Davis is also a skilled speaker, emphasizing psychological safety. She holds a Doctorate in Educational Psychology from the University of Southern California and an MBA from the University of Illinois, Champaign Urbana (Gies Business School).

Joyvina Evans, PhD is the Chair of the Online Master of Health Administration program and an Assistant Professor at Howard University in Washington, D.C. She has extensive experience in curriculum development for both traditional and competency-based education courses. Before taking on her full-time role in higher education, Dr Evans held various positions in both clinical and academic research. She holds a PhD and a Master of

Public Health, as well as a Master of Administration and a Bachelor of Business Administration. Dr Evans has also completed the Strategies for Higher Education Teaching and Learning program and the Women in Education Leadership program at Harvard University's Graduate School of Education. Additionally, she has earned certificates in Executive Leadership and High Performance from Cornell University. Dr Evans previously served as a quality reviewer for the Competency-Based Education Network (CBEN) and was a member of the Board of Directors for the Adult Higher Education Alliance (AHEA). She is an active member of the American Public Health Association, the Association of University Programs in Health Administration, and Alpha Kappa Alpha Sorority, Incorporated.

Rosalind Fleming, EdD is a visionary educational and community leader with over 15 years of experience advancing equity for Black children and educators. A former Principal and Heart of the Schools honoree, she is the Founder and Executive Director of Empowering Her Destiny, a nonprofit dedicated to equipping Black girls with the confidence and tools to thrive. Under her leadership, EHD has impacted over 100 Black girls through programs centered on mental health, mentorship, and self-advocacy. Dr Fleming is also the Founder of Unlocking Destiny, a consulting firm that partners with schools and organizations to build equitable, culturally responsive learning environments. A leadership coach and graduate of the Urban Educational Leadership Doctoral Program at Morgan State University, her research centers Black girls' lived experiences and aims to reframe how they are seen and supported. Through every facet of her work, Dr Fleming is committed to dismantling systemic barriers and helping Black girls and women step fully into their power.

Alexis Guethler, PhD, is an experienced online educator, researcher, and instructional designer at the University of Maryland School of Social Work. She earned her Doctorate in Instructional Technology from Towson University, with a primary focus on online course design and promoting student self-regulation. With academic roots in biology and K-12 education, Alexis has held various roles, including curriculum writing for informal educational programs, community college instruction, and faculty development. Specializing in designing curricula for a wide range of learners, Alexis emphasizes workforce pathways for nontraditional adult students. In addition to content creation, she is passionate about coaching faculty to leverage engaging and innovative technologies that align with their teaching goals. Alexis is an active member of the Association for Educational Communications and Technology and the International Association of Accessibility Professionals, committed to advancing inclusive and accessible educational practices through research and dissemination.

Jacqueline Hayden, is a dynamic Educational Consultant and founder of Ann Ignatius Solutions, LLC. She is also a doctoral candidate at Morgan State University in the Urban School Leadership Department. With over two decades of experience, she has served as an English teacher, Lead Teacher, Curriculum Specialist, Assistant Principal, and Principal in Washington, D.C. public and public charter schools. She later led as an Instructional Leadership Executive Director (Principal Supervisor) in Baltimore, MD, where she coached and mentored principals to advance instructional excellence and equity. A New Leaders, Emerging Leaders alumna and proud Washingtonian embraced by Baltimore, Jacque's leadership is marked by a fierce commitment to transformative practice and systemic change. Jacque's research at Morgan State focuses on the lived experiences of Black women principals, aligning with her broader mission to create affirming spaces for leaders of color. She is a grant manager and researcher for Sacred Stories, which documents the erased contributions of Black educators, particularly the legacy of Henriette DeLille and the Sisters of the Holy Family in New Orleans, LA. She also contributes to the Morgan State University's Urban Leaders Collective, helping reimagine leader preparation through a lens of Blackness and equity. Through her consulting, Jacque mentors and sponsors emerging Black women leaders, helping them thrive in systems not built for their success, while boldly insisting that access, opportunity, and joy are non-negotiable.

Jennifer Holland is the founder of SystemAlign, a consulting firm dedicated to aligning people, systems, and processes across various industries, including custom solutions for higher education. She has been serving higher education in various capacities since 2011, working directly with students, faculty, staff, and senior leadership. Her work in higher education encompasses program management, digital transformations and pedagogy, cultural transformations, and leadership development. She focuses on breaking down silos, fostering cross-collaborations within an assessment-driven community, and enhancing organizational effectiveness. Jennifer's experience includes project management, change management, stakeholder development and engagement, strategic systems alignment, and driving growth and development through customized interventions. Jennifer has served as both an internal and external consultant, leveraging her expertise in business, psychology, and behavioral science to develop proactive solutions that address challenges and drive positive outcomes.

La'Tonya "LT" Rease Miles, PhD: As a first-generation college graduate and thought leader in higher education, La'Tonya "LT" Rease Miles, PhD has been instrumental in establishing successful programs for first-gen students at both UCLA and Loyola Marymount University. In her many leadership roles, including her current role as Partnership Development

Representative at ReUp Education and co-founder of My Tribe Media, she advises institutions on first-gen student experiences. She regularly champions initiatives for nontraditional adult learners and contributes to scholarly discourse on first-gen experiences. Her influence extends to the digital sphere where she has co-founded several online communities, including a national Facebook group that empowers first-generation students. She earned a PhD in American literature from UCLA; and her research interests include the hidden curriculum in higher education, narratives about the first-generation college experience, and the representation of first-generation students in popular culture. Her most recent publication explores the positive relationships between campus service workers and first-generation students; and she is the co-editor of a forthcoming book about the Black first-generation experience. Further, LT is passionate about NBA basketball, college football, "Friday Night Lights," and "The Flash."

Merab Mushfiq works at Wilfrid Laurier University and is also completing her PhD in Education from York University. She has been working with students in higher education for the last 10 years and is very passionate about students' success, retention, and well-being.

Johnathon E. Paape, EdD, is an Academic Counselor and Success Coach for the Mechanical Engineering department at the University of Arkansas-Fayetteville. He holds a Doctor of Education in Adult and Lifelong Learning from the University of Arkansas and has worked with adult learners in various capacities for most of his career in higher education. Dr Paape is also currently on the editorial review boards for the National Academic Advising Association (NACADA) as well as the Journal of Student Affairs Research and Practice (JSARP). His research interests include community college placement policies, developmental education, retention and completion, and community college leadership.

Gretchen Rudham, EdD, is an Associate Professor of Urban Educational Leadership at her alma mater, Morgan State University where she educates Black educators and school leaders. Her research interests include Digital Humanities, Founding Black Educators, social justice leadership, and dismantling Whiteness in curriculum, schools, and society. Her most recent projects include three NEH grants: The Search for Founding Black Mothers K-12 Institute (2022), Buried Blueprints of Black Education HBCU Humanities Initiative (2024), and Humanities Collections and Reference Resources (2025) Sacred Stories: Digitizing the Sisters of the Holy Family Archives. She is also senior researcher on the Wallace Equity-Centered Principal Pathway grant team, founder of MSU doctoral students' Advisory Board Think Tank and the Urban Leaders Collective. Her recent publications include The Search for Founding Black Mothers: Digital Storytelling as Reclamation.

Darian Senn-Carter EdD, is Director and Professor of the Homeland Security and Criminal Justice Institute at Anne Arundel Community College (AACC). He is a nationally recognized leader, facilitating student engagement and success. Dr Senn-Carter serves as a Member of the Board of Directors for the Maryland Book Bank, Civic Works Inc., Reach Partnership School, Leaders of Tomorrow Youth Center, and CollegeBound Foundation Alumni Association. He is the founder and coordinator of the Aspiring Leaders Academy mentoring program, co-founder of the University of Maryland College Park Incentive Awards Visionary Scholarship Award, co-founder of the CollegeBound Foundation Alumni Scholarship Award, and co-founder of the Dunbar High School Alumni Scholarship Award. Dr Senn-Carter has served in many key leadership roles and is a recent recipient of several Awards. Dr Senn-Carter earned a Bachelor's Degree from the University of Maryland in Criminology and Criminal Justice, Master's Degree in Homeland Security and Post Baccalaureate Certificate in Security Assessment and Management from Towson University and a Doctorate Degree in Education from Edgewood College. Dr Senn-Carter is a certified Life Coach (International Coach Federation), licensed Emergency Medical Technician, obtained a Teaching Certificate in Special Education, and has completed numerous courses and training in leadership and education. He has participated in conferences, workshops, presentations, and panel discussions both regionally and nationally.

Sharon Ultsch is an intrepid life-long learner. She has been an adult educator in diverse educational and community settings for over 30 years. After a Peace Corps tour in Ecuador as a faculty developer, she became a senior lecturer in the Department of Education at the University of Vermont (UVM). She has developed and facilitated a variety of educational development workshops to international audiences. She received her Doctorate in Education from UVM's Educational Leadership and Policy Program. Her current scholarship interests are equity in assessment, critical pedagogy in higher education, and critical university studies.

Stacy Ybarra Evans is a native of San Antonio, Texas. Since 2014, Stacy has been Director of Student Engagement for Catch the Next and has responsible for social media outreach for the program and also co-director of the program's Transfer Motivational Program. She currently works as an adjunct instructor teaching the learning frameworks and student development courses at San Antonio College, one of San Antonio's oldest colleges. She enjoys enriching learning opportunities and recently graduated from the Master Teacher Certification and Certified Adjunct certification programs at the Alamo Colleges. She has worked for the Alamo Colleges for 16 years with her current role working with the guided pathways initiative—transfer advising guides. Her main focus is on community collaboration which has led her to a number of community collaborations and into community leadership participation as a member of the first Leadership SAISD cohort and member of the second cohort of the San Antonio Hispanic Chamber of Commerce's Latina Leadership Institute. She completed NASPA's 2016 Escaleras Institute—*Latinx/a/o Student Affairs Professionals Scaling New Heights in Leadership* is designed for Latinx/a/o student affairs professionals who aspire to senior student affairs officer roles. She now currently serves as a board member for NASPA's Center for Women.

INTRODUCTION

Darian Senn-Carter

Higher education institutions are finding new, creative, and innovative ways to support adult learners. To capture some of the unique ways that practitioners are doing this, this book delves into the transformative practices and evolving challenges within higher education, focusing on strategies to enhance adult learner success and drive organizational change. Higher education institutions occupy a unique and indispensable role in today's educational landscape, particularly in their mission to serve diverse adult learners seeking to enhance their skills and pursue academic and career goals.

At the heart of this exploration is a commitment to addressing key challenges faced by educators, such as accurately assessing student readiness, supporting first-generation and adult learners, and adapting pedagogical approaches to meet diverse student needs. By examining these challenges through the lens of innovation and equity, this book aims to provide actionable insights and evidence-based strategies that educators can leverage to drive positive change.

Throughout the chapters, three overarching themes emerge

1. **Redefining Success Through Assessment**: We delve into the evolution of assessment practices, emphasizing the shift towards multiple measures assessments that consider holistic indicators of student potential beyond traditional standardized tests.
2. **Supporting Diverse Learners**: Highlighting the importance of inclusive practices, this book explores initiatives aimed at supporting first-generation, international, and adult learners, ensuring equitable access to educational opportunities.
3. **Promoting Flexibility and Innovation**: Recognizing the dynamic needs of adult learners, this book examines innovative pedagogical strategies, flexible learning formats, and institutional transformations that enhance educational access, engagement, and outcomes.

Guided by principles of equity, student-centeredness, and continuous improvement, we seek to inspire collaborative efforts to advance the adult learners' experience. By showcasing effective practices and evidence-based research, we aim to empower readers with practical tools and insights to foster a culture of innovation, inclusivity, and excellence in higher education. Ultimately, this book serves as a call to action to embrace innovation, cultivate equity, and prioritize student success. Through collective effort and shared commitment, we can continue to propel higher education forward, in shaping a more accessible, equitable, and prosperous future.

Theme 1: Redefining Success Through Multiple Measures Assessments

The first theme explores innovative approaches to assessing adult learners' readiness for college-level coursework. In this theme, the focus is on exploring how practitioners are redefining their approaches to student assessment. Traditional methods often relied heavily on standardized tests, which may not fully capture the potential and readiness of diverse adult learners. The theme examines the shift towards multiple measures assessments (MMAs), which consider a broader range of factors such as high school performance, noncognitive skills, and lived and learned experiences. By embracing MMAs, practitioners and higher education institutions aim to more accurately place students into appropriate courses and support their success in college-level coursework. This theme also explores the impact of MMAs on improving retention and graduation rates, and overall student outcomes. This evolution not only enhances placement accuracy but also promotes equitable access to higher education, while acknowledging and valuing the adult learner holistically.

Theme 2: Supporting Diverse Learners and Pedagogical Innovation

The second theme delves into pedagogical innovations aimed at empowering faculty and supporting diverse student populations. This theme highlights the imperative of supporting the diverse demographic of adult students within higher education. It explores innovative programs, support services, and policies designed to enhance equity and inclusivity in higher education. Key topics include mentorship programs for students, culturally responsive teaching practices, language support services for international students, and tailored academic advising for adult learners returning to education. The theme underscores the importance of creating an inclusive learning environment that addresses the unique needs and challenges faced by diverse student populations.

Theme 3: Flexibility and Adaptability in Higher Education

The third theme emphasizes flexibility as a cornerstone of success for adult learners. The theme of promoting flexibility and innovation centers on how community colleges are adapting their educational models and institutional practices to better serve learners and respond to evolving educational landscapes. This includes exploring flexible learning pathways such as online courses, hybrid formats, competency-based education, and credit for prior learning. Additionally, this theme delves into the role of technology in enhancing learning experiences, fostering digital literacy skills, and supporting personalized learning journeys. Institutional innovations such as the establishment of teaching excellence centers, collaborative learning spaces, and partnerships with industries are also examined to illustrate how community colleges are driving educational excellence and responsiveness.

Moreover, this book advocates for continuous innovation and adaptation within higher education to meet the evolving needs of learners. By embracing multiple measures assessments, enhancing pedagogical practices, and fostering flexibility, institutions can drive positive change and empower adult students from diverse backgrounds to achieve their academic and professional aspirations. This compilation of experiences and strategies provides a comprehensive exploration of the role of higher education in shaping the future of adult education. It is our hope that the insights and strategies shared here will inspire educators to collaborate in creating inclusive and transformative learning environments for adult learners.

SECTION 1

REDEFINING SUCCESS THROUGH MULTIPLE
MEASURES ASSESSMENTS

CHAPTER 1

ADULT LEARNER SUCCESS IN COMMUNITY COLLEGES: IMPROVING OUTCOMES USING MULTIPLE MEASURES ASSESSMENTS

Johnathon E. Paape
University of Arkansas-Fayetteville, USA

ABSTRACT

Adult learners often choose community colleges as a place to begin their educational journey due to their low cost and relatively quick credential opportunities. However, many students face barriers to their education due to placement into noncredit remedial coursework that can add unnecessary time to a student's college career. Due to the often-lengthy nature of remedial courses, adult learners become delayed in getting to core college-level math and English courses, further delaying their graduation and increasing chances of attrition. Standardized placement tests have historically been used to determine placement of students into college-level courses; however, there is research that shows that these tests be inaccurate leading to misplacement. In response to these outcomes (as well as issues related to the pandemic), many researchers and state policymakers have pushed for the use of multiple measures assessments (MMAs) as an alternative to single-test placement policies. This chapter will examine adult-learners in context of the community college, problems with single-test placement policies, how these policies affect adult learners, and the benefits of MMAs on future adult learner success.

Keywords: Adult learning; multiple measures assessment; remedial education; developmental education; community college; placement policies; standardized tests

INTRODUCTION

Since their inception, community colleges have been designed around educating more traditional-aged students rather than their adult counterparts. In fact, the first community colleges created were done so to act as extensions of high school as well as to offer an alternative pathway for non-university-bound students (Kisker et al., 2023; Thelin, 2011). Even today, many of the mechanisms, policies, and class structures provided by community colleges generally tend to focus on students entering as freshmen from high school. Bahr et al. (2021) discussed that adult learners "...often need or benefit from program structures and support systems than [sic] differ from those offered by colleges and oriented toward younger students" (p. 3). This discrepancy is unusual when you consider that adult learners (students age 25+) comprise just under one-third (31%) of all community college students (calculated by author using data from Jenkins & Fink, 2020 (updated Jan. 2024)). Hussar and Bailey (2017) predicted that students aged 25 and older would comprise around 9.7 million students by 2025. While this number is still lower than traditional student enrollment, it is predicted that students ages 25 to 34 and 35 years and older will increase 16 and 20%, respectively, between 2014 and 2025 (Hussar and Bailey, 2017). With decreased enrollments due to the COVID-19 pandemic coupled with expected decreases in first-time, traditional students due to low high school graduation rates and declining birth rates, this increase means that it is crucial for community colleges to adapt quickly to serve the adult population.

An issue, though, is that due to the dominant structure of higher education, many adult learners encounter barriers to their education at all levels of their college career. One such barrier is that adult learners often enter college assessed as being academically underprepared for college-level coursework. Colleges have typically relied on standardized tests (e.g. ACT, SAT, Accuplacer) to determine student readiness for college-level math and English courses; however, there is evidence that not only are these tests potentially inaccurate, but they also have a high rate of misplacement. This means that many adult learners that are placed into remedial coursework are done so despite the high likelihood they could pass college-level coursework. Even more troubling is the fact that adult learners are often highly represented in remedial courses (Bailey et al., 2015; National Center for Education; Scott-Clayton et al., 2014; Statistics, 2023). This is especially true for women and underrepresented racial minorities (Bahr, 2010; Crisp & Delgado, 2014; Scott-Clayton et al., 2014). To combat this, many researchers, state legislatures, and state boards of higher education have begun to push for changes in policy that would eliminate college reliant use of the tests as the only factors for placement. The fruits of these labors have proliferated throughout community colleges in the form of Multiple Measures Assessments (MMAs) (Rutschow et al., 2019). Generally speaking, MMAs are the use of multiple factors to determine student readiness for college-level coursework. MMAs can take many forms, but the most common three are decision rule, decision band, and algorithmic models (Bickerstaff et al., 2021). Decision rule models use multiple options to determine placement, passing any one of which can be used to allow students into college-level coursework (Bickerstaff et al., 2021). Decision band models have specified score ranges that are used. When students exceed the scores in a range, they are placed into college-level coursework. Those who fall below the range are placed into remedial work, with those scoring within the range moving to evaluation on different factors (Bickerstaff et al., 2021). Last, algorithmic models evaluate students based on historical data to examine all factors at the same time. The result of this is an algorithm that (...combines and weights incoming students' values on selected measures to establish a placement score for each student" (Bickerstaff et al., 2021, p. 2). Though each model has its value for different institutional situations, the most common model-type is algorithmic due to its ability to be easily adjusted using continuously updated historical data. However, all of these models can contribute to reducing student remediation, especially for more vulnerable populations that are found to be placed into remediation at higher rates such as adult learners and students of color.

ADULT LEARNERS AND REMEDIAL EDUCATION

Students that enter college and are deemed "underprepared" for college-level coursework are often referred to remedial education as a remedy. For many years, this status was determined by how well students did on high-stakes placement exams. An issue, though, is that many students, especially adult learners who have never been to college or are returning after a long hiatus, may not understand the importance of these tests or lack preparation time (Bailey et al., 2015; Fay et al., 2013). As a result, adult learners and other nontraditional students, as well as underrepresented students of color, are often greatly overrepresented in college remedial coursework (Bahr, 2010; Bailey et al., 2015; National Center for Education; Paape, 2022; Scott-Clayton et al., 2014; Statistics, 2023). With low completion rates among adult students in the courses, this affects not only student retention but also completion.

According to the National Center for Education Statistics (2022), since 2003, 31.4% of students that attended college have taken at least one remedial course. For community colleges specifically, the share of remedial students rises to 38.2%. Overall, for adult students, approximately 73% (33.6% for 24–29; 35.4% for 30+) have taken at least one remedial course. Similar disparities exist between race/ethnicity populations when compared to White students.

Before efforts were made to begin restructuring how we actually place students into remedial courses, many colleges and researchers were focused on restructuring the courses themselves. A popular method that came from these efforts was to make the switch away from lengthy pre-requisite sequences and replace them with a co-requisite model that allowed students to take remedial work and the corresponding college-level course together (Scott-Clayton, 2018; Zhao et al., 2022). This is a great position for colleges to adopt considering that Bailey et al. (2008) found that "...only one third to two fifths of students referred to developmental education actually complete their entire developmental sequence" (p. 2) and that "...about two thirds of students who fail to complete the sequence to which they were referred do so even while having passed all of the developmental courses in which they enrolled" (p. 3). Co-requisite models have shortened this time in an effort to reduce unnecessary sequences and get students through the corresponding college course faster, thus increasing their chances of both attempting the course and, hopefully, passing it (Bailey et al., 2015). This shift, in tandem with the implementation of MMAs, greatly assists students who still happen to need remedial coursework by reducing the time it takes to get through remedial courses, thus potentially shortening time to graduation.

Though a great number of students are referred to remedial courses each year, more are referred to math than are to English. Research conducted by Bailey et al. (2008) showed that 59% and 33% of students were referred to math and English, respectively. More recently, in an examination of Florida's developmental policies changes, Zhao et al. (2022) found that after policy implementation, 18.34% of students still needed remedial English compared to 30.34% of students who needed remedial math. This is important to note as math is commonly considered a "gatekeeper" course in colleges, often preventing many students from continuing in their educational journeys.

In terms of overall numbers, more recently, a report from the National Center for Education Statistics (NCESs) found that approximately 40% of all students attending two-year, public institutions took at least one remedial course (National Center for Education Statistics, 2023). The same report also showed that underrepresented students of color as well as adult learners are significantly impacted by this. Black (50%), Hispanic or Latino (45%), Asian (41%), and Native Hawaiian/Pacific Islander (44%) were all found to take remedial courses at higher rates than White (35%) students (National Center for Education Statistics, 2023).

PROBLEMS WITH REMEDIAL PLACEMENT METHODS

Retention and graduation issues are a main concern within community colleges. As of the 2019 cohort, the average graduation rate for community colleges was 35.5% (National Center for Education Statistics, 2022b). Many of the woes community colleges face in this area are self-inflicted; that is, some of the reasons for retention issues stem from the high number of students the colleges place into remedial coursework who then go on to not complete that sequence's college-level course, let alone a degree. Colleges have traditionally relied on high-stakes standardized placement tests as the primary determinant of whether a student will be able to enroll in college-level math and English courses. As noted by Counterman and Zientek (2022), "Placement tests are considered high-stake assessments because scores can alter students' paths to college completion" (p. 1). These can take the form of prepackaged tests or tests created and assessed by college faculty for the use of placement. Because many adult learners have large gaps between high school (or GED) completion and beginning college, it is often believed that they would not be successful in college-level courses due to skills degradation. However, many of these conclusions are based on historical reliance on a single score from these placement tests which don't measure these students in a more holistic manner.

Of course, for adult learners who may not have taken any math or English course in a number of years, these tests present certain issues related to how students perceive/prepare for them. Many times, adult learners don't understand that these tests will be used to place them into coursework. As a result, they may not prepare as well as they could. Other main concerns, as discussed by Bailey et al. (2015), include:

> First, most incoming students are unaware of the purpose and consequences of the placement tests…Second, placement test content is often poorly aligned with academic standards and expectations of college-level coursework. Third, and perhaps most important, the skills that can be tested on a short multiple-choice test represent only a small subset of those needed to be successful in college. (p. 127)

Other major concerns of these exams range from their overall predictive accuracy to the sheer number of students erroneously misplaced by them

(Belfield & Crosta, 2012; Paape, 2022; Scott-Clayton, 2012; Scott-Clayton et al., 2014). Through their own research, College Board reports extremely low correlations between the Accuplacer exam and math and English outcomes (Mattern & Packman, 2009). Scott-Clayton (2012) found that the sole use of placement exams led to severe misplacement of students into remedial math and English. Research has also found that, when considering other factors such as HS GPA, any predictive power from placement tests is often reduced to nonsignificant levels (Belfield & Crosta, 2012; Paape, 2022; Scott-Clayton et al., 2012)

Effects on Underserved Populations

As mentioned, adults are often disproportionately represented in remedial coursework. This is especially true for students of color who often are placed into and successfully complete these courses at far lower rates than White students (Bahr, 2010; Chen & Simone, 2016; Scott-Clayton et al., 2014). Bahr (2010) found that White students enrolled in remedial courses were more likely to complete them than Black or Hispanic students (3.1 and 1.6 times, respectively). Similarly, Chen and Simone (2016) found that among students examined that began at two-year institutions, 78.3% of Black students and 74.9% of Hispanic students took remedial courses in any field compared to 63.6% of White students. The same study also found that Black and Hispanic students tend to take a higher average number of remedial courses, with Black and Hispanic students found to take 4.0 and 3.5 courses, respectively, compared to 2.4 courses taken by White students (Chen & Simone, 2016). However, it is important to note that "...race itself is not a *cause* of the disparities; rather, it is the many correlated facets of inequality that lead to lower preparation and achievement among historically disadvantaged racial groups" (Bahr, 2010, p. 212).

USING MMAS TO IMPROVE ADULT LEARNER SUCCESS

In simple terms, MMAs are the use of multiple factors to assess a student's potential to pass college-level courses. They have emerged as a viable replacement for test-only policies, showing promising results on student outcomes in both course and degree completion. While institutions seemed to lag in adapting these models to replace test-only policies, they were given special attention during the COVID-19 pandemic due to many testing sites closing. As a result, colleges were forced to find alternative placement methods to accommodate students who wished to attend school during the pandemic. These models can include variables that allow for a more complete picture of a student such as high school GPA, courses taken in high school, and time since high school, as well as non cognitive variables such as GRIT or motivation (Bahr, 2016; Bahr et al., 2019; Belfield & Crosta, 2012; Bergman et al., 2021; Cullinan & Kopko, 2022; Ngo & Kwon, 2015; Woods et al., 2018; Scott-Clayton et al., 2012). Much of this research has also shown that high school GPA is most commonly the highest predictor of success for students.

Though MMAs have been shown to increase overall student outcomes, adult learners can especially stand to benefit from these new policies. Between 2003 and 2020, the number of first-year undergraduate students aged 24+ enrolled in any remedial courses (among all institution levels) was approximately 69% (NCES, 2022, Table 331.40). With so many adult learners enrolling in remedial courses, coupled with the fact that many of these students don't complete that remedial work, it is important to utilize methods that reduce the need for remedial coursework and lead to higher rates of persistence and credential completion for this population. Kopko and Daniels (2023) found that "…program group students in the bump-up zone in math or English were about 9 percentage points more likely to complete a college-level math or English courses (with a C or higher) within nine terms" (p. 7).

These improvements to placement also heavily benefit students of color. Using an algorithmic placement model, Bergman et al. (2021) found that Black and Hispanic students both had significant improvements to placement in college-level courses (at different rates) compared to White students. They also note that "…though all students seem to benefit from algorithmic placement, there is evidence that most (though, not all) of the benefits accrue to students traditionally under-represented in college courses" (Bergman et al., 2021, p. 24).

THE CURRENT LANDSCAPE OF PLACEMENT

Multiple measures have received more attention in recent years as a means to improve student outcomes in higher education. These efforts were undoubtedly sped-up due to testing sites closing during the COVID-19 pandemic. Before the pandemic, many community colleges relied on a single measure to place students, often using standardized tests (Rutschow et al., 2019). Since then, however, a "…majority of states (37) address DE placement through statewide or system wide policy…" with "…18 of the 37 states with DE assessment…" requiring a version of MMAs (Hodges et al., 2020, p. 4). While this increase cannot be causally linked to the pandemic given that great strides were already underway by researchers, administrators, and legislators to address remedial placement concerns, it can be inferred that it accounted for some of the shown increases.

Though states have begun to accept MMAs into state policy to address student outcomes, how states approach defining MMAs varies. Hodges et al. (2020) discussed that:

> One state policy may mandate multiple measures placement based on cognitive and noncognitive measures or based on a standardized test score considered in conjunction with other measures...Some states, however, mandate a multiple measures placement based on a student meeting only one of several criteria listed.... (p. 4)

As a result, marked improvements from using MMAs have been seen in student outcomes including course completion, number of credits earned, and graduation (Bergman et al., 2021; Kopko & Daniels, 2023; Zhao et al., 2022). California, for example, enacted Assembly Bill 705 which mandated that colleges in the state no longer use test-only policies, but instead focus on other factors that include high school information (Ganga & Mazzariello, 2019; Ngo & Melguizo, 2022). From this, many researchers have found improvements to students' completion of college-level math and English courses compared to students who take remedial courses (Bracco et al., 2021; Bahr et al., 2019; Ngo & Melguizo, 2022). In Florida, Senate Bill 1720 was passed which required more than one measure to be assessed to reduce the number of students assessed as needing developmental coursework (Zhao et al., 2022). So far, the results of this have been promising with Zhao et al. (2022) finding "significantly higher percentages of students enrolling in and completing college-level and advanced English and math courses after the reform" (p. 171). Though not all states' reforms can be covered here, it is notable that excellent progress has been made by states and colleges to increase access to college-level coursework.

DISCUSSION AND RECOMMENDATIONS FOR PRACTICE

To assist adult learners in accessing important first-year math and English courses, community colleges need to carefully re-examine their placement policies, especially those that still include examining test scores as a means of placement. Because standardized tests only provide a snapshot of a student's perceived skills at a particular point-in-time, they miss many of the other factors that could show adult learner potential for higher academic work. As an example, adult learners are often associated as being more mature than traditional-aged college students. This maturity might lead an adult to put more effort into learning the needed math and English skills to successfully complete a college-level course. In examining non-traditional students, Paape (2022) found that "time since high school" was a positive predictor of non-traditional student success in College Algebra.

As part of their examination, college administrators should explore their own college's data, coupled with theory and research, to determine what measures work at their institution. With research showing that placement test scores are often lowly correlated with success in college-level math and English, as well as the fact that many adult learners tend not to do well on placement tests for reasons explored in this chapter, colleges would be well-suited to remove these tests from consideration all-together in MMAs. Instead, colleges should focus on HS GPA as a main predictive factor when assessing student readiness. Other non-cognitive measures such as motivation or GRIT should also be examined since these measures have been shown to benefit adult learners' placement into college-level courses.

In order to better assist those who would still be placed into remedial coursework that colleges quickly move away from pre-requisite models of remediation and embrace co-requisite models. With research showing that many students do not complete the lengthy pre-requisite sequences, especially for math, moving to co-requisite models can reduce the time to college-level courses. This move may also increase persistence and degree attainment of those needing remediation. Chen and Simone (2016) found that students at two-year institutions who completed their remedial coursework and went on to pass the respective college-level course, 26% obtained an associate's degree compared to 12% of non-completers.

This would also serve community colleges looking to recruit adult learners to fill declining enrollments from first-time, traditional students. Since many students that are initially placed into remedial coursework do not complete the sequence and eventually drop-out, colleges attempting to recruit former students that did not complete a program may be able to better position those students to avoid remedial work due to MMAs.

In addition, state boards of higher education and state legislators need to take more direct action to assist community colleges in establishing MMAs. As was discussed in this chapter, though there are states that have introduced legislation prohibiting colleges from making placement decisions based only on single-test policies, there are more states that are not as directly involved. States moving to require MMAs in any form along with boards of higher education assisting colleges in identifying relevant variables of interest will be needed to achieve student outcome goals.

CONCLUSION

As was explored in this chapter, alternative placement models such as MMAs have great potential to allow adult learners earlier access to college-level courses and reduce placement into remedial coursework. With community colleges' mission of increasing social mobility for those whom they serve, MMAs have shown that they can directly serve this mission by leading to faster access to critical college-level math and English courses, which in-turn can assist with retention and completion issues. This also serves to align with many community colleges' mission regarding serving a diverse student base. As discussed above, underrepresented students of color are highly represented in remedial courses. Much of the research that exists on MMAs consistently shows that these models improve placement opportunities for these students, a critical step in increasing degree attainment for this population, thus hopefully decreasing the existing equity gap. To make the strides, though, states will need to be more involved in passing legislative measures that move colleges toward multiple measures placement. Colleges will also need to be more proactive and involved in making these changes to align with recommendations (and evidence) from researchers in the field. Hopefully, as we move beyond the pandemic and as research on MMAs increases, administrators and state parties can work together to create systems that not only support student outcomes, but also challenge pre-existing structures of inequity that exist that often keep adult learners and students of color from attaining their college goals.

REFERENCES

Bahr, P. R. (2010). Preparing the underprepared: An analysis of racial disparities in postsecondary mathematics remediation. *The Journal of Higher Education, 81*(2), 209–237. https://doi.org/10.1080/00221546.2010.11779049

Bahr, P. R. (2016). *Replacing placement tests in Michigan's community colleges.* Center for the Study of Higher and Postsecondary Education, University of Michigan.

Bahr, P. R., Boeck, C. A., & Cummins, P. A. (2021). Strengthening outcomes of adult students in community colleges. In L. W. Perna (Ed.), *Higher education: Handbook of theory and research* (Vol. 36, pp. 1–57). Springer. https://doi.org/10.1007/978-3-030- 43030- 6_3-2

Bahr, P. R., Fagioli, L. P., Hetts, J., Hayward, C., Willett, T., Lamoree, D., & Baker, R. B. (2019). Improving placement accuracy in California's community colleges using multiple measures of high school achievement. *Community College Review, 47*(2), 178–211.

Bailey, T., Jaggars, S. S., & Jenkins, D. (2015). *Redesigning America's community colleges.* Harvard University Press.

Bailey, T., Jeong, D. W., & Cho, S. W. (2008). *Referral, enrollment, and completion in developmental education sequences in community colleges.* CCRC Working Paper No. 15. Community College Research Center, Columbia University.

Belfield, C. R., & Crosta, P. M. (2012). *Predicting success in college: The importance of placement tests and high school transcripts* CCRC Working Paper No. 42. Community College Research Center, Columbia University.workpap

Bergman, P., Kopko, E., & Rodriguez, J. (2021). *Using predictive analytics to track students: Evidence from a seven-college experiment* CESifo Working Paper No. 9157. https://doi.org/10.2139/ssrn.3875991workpap

Bickerstaff, S., Kopko, E., Lewy, E. B., Raufman, J., & Rutschow, E. Z. (2021). *Implementing and scaling multiple measures assessment in the context of COVID-19.* Research Brief. Center for the Analysis of Postsecondary Readiness.

Bracco, K. R., Huang, C. W., Fong, T., & Finkelstein, N. (2021). Using multiple measures to predict success in students' first college math course: An examination of multiple measures under executive order 1110 in the California state university system. *West Ed.* https://eric.ed.gov/?id=ED616073

Chen, X., & Simone, S. (2016). *Remedial coursetaking at US public 2-and 4-year institutions: Scope, experiences, and outcomes* Statistical Analysis Report. NCES 2016-405. National Center for Education Statistics. https://files.eric.ed.gov/fulltext/ED568682.pdfreport

Counterman, C., & Zientek, L. R. (2022). High school transcript placement in developmental mathematics courses: A case study at one college. *European Journal of Science and Mathematics Education, 10*(3), 1–14. https://doi.org/10.30935/scimath/12430

Crisp, G., & Delgado, C. (2014). The impact of developmental education on community college persistence and vertical transfer. *Community College Review, 42*(2), 99–117. https://www.proquest.com/scholarly-journals/impact-developmental-education-oncommunity/docview/1518507453/se-?accountid=8361

Cullinan, D., & Kopko, E. M. (2022). *Lessons from two experimental studies of multiple measures assessment* Center for the Analysis of Postsecondary Readiness. Community College Research Center, Columbia University. https://ccrc.tc.columbia.edu/media/k2/attachments/multiple-measures-assessmentreflections.pdf

Fay, M. P., Bickerstaff, S., & Hodara, M. (2013). *Why students do not prepare for math placement exams: Student perspectives.* CCRC Research Brief. Number 57. Community College Research Center, Columbia University.

Ganga, E., & Mazzariello, A. (2019). Modernizing college course placement by using multiple measures. *Education Commission of the States.* https://doi.org/10.7916/d8-fa8c-py77

Hodges, R., Payne, E. M., McConnell, M. C., Lollar, J., Guckert, D. A., Owens, S., Gonzales, C., Hoff, M. A., Lussier, K. O., Wu, N., & Shinn, H. B. (2020). Developmental education policy and reforms: A 50-state snapshot. *Journal of Developmental Education, 44*(1), 2–17. http://www.jstor.org/stable/45381092

Hussar, W. J., & Bailey, T. M. (2017). *Projections of education statistics to 2025. NCES 2017-019.* National Center for Education Statistics. https://files.eric.ed.gov/fulltext/ED576296.pdf

Jenkins, D., & Fink, J. (2020). How will COVID-19 affect community college enrollment? Looking to the great recession for clues. *The Mixed Methods Blog.* https://ccrc.tc.columbia.edu/easyblog/covid-community-college-enrollment.html

Kisker, C. B., Cohen, A. M., & Brawer, F. B. (2023). *The American community college.* John Wiley & Sons.

Kopko, E., & Daniels, H. (2023). The long-term effects of multiple measures assessment at SUNY community colleges. *Center for the Analysis of Postsecondary Readiness.* https://eric.ed.gov/?id=ED632528

Kopko, E., Daniels, H., & Cullinan, D. (2023). The long-term effectiveness of multiple measures assessment: Evidence from a randomized controlled trial. *Center for the Analysis of Postsecondary Readiness.* https://ccrc.tc.columbia.edu/media/k2/attachments/long-term-effectiveness-multiple-measures-assessment.pdf

Mattern, K. D., & Packman, S. (2009). *Predictive validity of ACCUPLACER© scores for course placement: A meta-analysis* Research Report No. 2009-2. College Board. https://files.eric.ed.gov/fulltext/ED561046.pdf

National Center for Education Statistics. (2022b). Trends generator. *National Center for Education Statistics.* https://nces.ed.gov/ipeds/trendgenerator/app/answer/7/21

National Center for Education Statistics [NCES]. (2022). *Percentage of first-year undergraduate students who reported taking remedial education courses, by selected student and institution characteristics: Selected academic years, 2003-04 through 2019-20.* Digest of Education Statistics. https://nces.ed.gov/programs/digest/d22/tables/dt22_311.40.asp

National Center for Education Statistics. (2023). 2019-20 National postsecondary student aid study (NPSAS:20) https://nces.ed.gov/pubs2024/2024482.pdf

Ngo, F., & Kwon, W. W. (2015). Using multiple measures to make math placement decisions: Implications for access and success in community colleges. *Research in Higher Education, 56*(5), 442–470. https://doi.org/10.1007/s11162-014-9352-9

Ngo, Federick, & Melguizo, Tatiana (2022). *Mandating multiple measures and encouraging student supports: Evaluating a new approach to developmental education in California's community colleges* Ed Working Paper (pp. 22–662). https://doi.org/10.26300/neqq-gd84

Paape, J. E. (2022). *Improving math placement of non-traditional students in Arkansas community colleges using multiple measures assessment* Publication No. 29999630. Doctoral dissertation. University of Arkansas. ProQuest Dissertations & Theses Global.thesis

Rutschow, E. Z., Cormier, M. S., Dukes, D., & Zamora, D. E. C. (2019). *The changing landscape of developmental education practices: Findings from a national survey and interviews with postsecondary institutions.* Center for the Analysis of Postsecondary Readiness.

Scott-Clayton, J. (2012). *Do high-stakes placement exams predict college success?* CCRC Working Paper No. 41. Community College Research Center, Columbia University.workpap

Scott-Clayton, J. (2018). *Evidence-based reforms in college remediation are gaining steam and so far living up to the hype.* Brookings Institute. https://www.brookings.edu/rsearch/evidence-based-reforms-in-college-remediation-are gaining-steam-and-so-far-living-up-to-the-hype/

Scott-Clayton, J., Crosta, P. M., & Belfield, C. R. (2014). Improving the targeting of treatment: Evidence from college remediation. *Education Evaluation and Policy Analysis, 36*(3), 371–393. https://doi.org/10.3102/0162379713517935

Thelin, J. R. (2011). *A history of American higher education.* JHU Press.

Woods, C. S., Park, T., Shouping, H., & Betrand, J. T. (2018). How high school coursework predicts introductory college-level course success. *Community College Review, 46*(2), 176–196. https://doi.org/10.1177/0091552118759419

Zhao, K., Park-Gaghan, T. J., Mokhe, C. G., & Hu, S. (2022). Examining the impacts of Florida's developmental education reform for non-exempt students: The case of first-year English and math course enrollment and success. *Community College Review, 50*(2), 171–192.

CHAPTER 2

TRANSFORMING PEDAGOGY AND EMPOWERING FACULTY: THE IMPACT OF A CENTER FOR TEACHING EXCELLENCE ON ADULT EDUCATION

Stacy Ybarra Evans
San Antonio College, USA

ABSTRACT

This chapter illuminates the transformative potential of a Center for Teaching Excellence in enhancing adult education, drawing from the successful model at Our Lady of the Lake University. Through a multifaceted approach encompassing onboarding, workshops, coaching, and partnerships, faculty are empowered to master adult learning principles, cultivate inclusive classrooms, and refine teaching methodologies. The result is a tangible improvement in student engagement, learning outcomes, and overall success.

Central to this transformation is the continual process of assessment, with a spotlight on the pivotal role of diversity, equity, inclusion, and anti-racism in achieving excellence in adult education. Rooted in transformative learning theory and guided by adult learning principles, the chapter offers actionable recommendations for fostering equity and combating racism within educational settings.

Keywords: Adult education; CTE; faculty development; transformative learning; inclusive pedagogy; DEIA

NARRATIVE

As a dynamic leader dedicated to fostering student success and advancing inclusive practices in adult education, my work and research directly intersect with diversity, equity, inclusion, and anti-racism (DEIA) within the contexts of adult education. In my role as the Director of the Center for Teaching Excellence (CTE) at Our Lady of the Lake University, I spearhead initiatives aimed at empowering faculty to create inclusive learning environments that prioritize DEIA principles. An example of these initiatives are two specific roles that work alongside the CTE as part of the Idea in Action Grant. In the role of a faculty leader, the responsibility of applying for a course release and stipend to facilitate workshops on diversity, equity, and inclusion (DEI) topics such as walking methodologies falls under their purview. In this capacity, they leverage their expertise to not only lead these workshops but also to cultivate an environment where faculty members are empowered to integrate DEI principles into their teaching practices. By offering resources, support, and incentives, they aim to foster a community of educators committed to creating inclusive and culturally responsive learning experiences for all students. Separately, the **First-Year and Second-Year Coordinator** is entrusted with the pivotal task of orchestrating DEI training sessions for both faculty and staff. Additionally, they undertake the redesign of the first-year seminar and the university's flight school, which serves as a crucial on-boarding program for students before they embark on their academic journey. Through these initiatives, they strive to create an inclusive and welcoming campus environment where all students feel valued and supported in their educational pursuits. By infusing DEI principles into every aspect of the curriculum and student experience, they endeavor to cultivate a culture of belonging and academic success for every member of the university community. Through strategic leadership, I advocate for transformative pedagogical approaches that cater to the diverse needs of adult learners, ensuring equitable access to education for all individuals, regardless of their backgrounds. This includes developing and implementing comprehensive onboarding programs, hosting workshops focused on inclusive teaching practices, providing personalized coaching to faculty members, and fostering collaborative partnerships to promote DEIA values across the institution.

In addition to my institutional role, I actively engage in shaping transfer pathways and supporting student success within the broader educational community, advocating for systemic changes that promote equity and inclusion. By emphasizing ongoing assessment and the integration of DEIA principles into all aspects of adult education, I strive to create a culture of continuous improvement and accountability. My commitment to DEIA extends beyond my institution, as I also serve as an adjunct faculty member at San Antonio College and contribute to educational initiatives within the

Alamo Colleges District. Through these roles, I actively shape transfer pathways and support student success while advocating for inclusive practices.

In essence, my professional endeavors exemplify my unwavering commitment to promoting DEIA within adult education. Through my visionary leadership and innovative practices, I continue to inspire positive change and elevate the educational experience for students and educators alike.

DR. YBARRA'S WORK AND DEIA IN ADULT EDUCATION

As the Director of the CTE at Our Lady of the Lake University, the utilization of Transformative Learning Theory (TLT) has been instrumental in shaping my approach to adult education. TLT, developed by Jack Mezirow, serves as a foundational framework for analyzing experiences and research in the field of teaching and learning. Mezirow (1997) defines transformative learning as a process where individuals use their existing interpretations to construct new meanings from their experiences, guiding their future actions. This theory suggests that learning can be transformative, challenging individuals' assumptions, fostering personal growth, and promoting social change.

In my role, I have found that creating a safe and supportive environment for learners is paramount in facilitating transformative learning experiences. Following Cranton's (1994) emphasis on the educator's role, I strive to encourage learners to challenge their assumptions, engage in open dialogue, and feel empowered to explore new perspectives. Central to TLT are concepts such as critical reflection, disorienting dilemmas, meaning making, and empowerment. Critical reflection allows learners to examine their assumptions, biases, and experiences to understand how these factors shape their perspectives. Disorienting dilemmas disrupt established worldviews, prompting learners to question their beliefs and consider new perspectives. Meaning making involves synthesizing new understandings from experiences and integrating them into existing knowledge. Empowerment, a key aspect of transformative learning, leads to increased self-awareness, the ability to challenge the status quo, and the potential to contribute to positive social change.

In my practice, I have found that incorporating these elements of TLT into professional development programs for faculty members has been particularly effective. By encouraging critical reflection, providing opportunities for experiencing disorienting dilemmas, facilitating meaning making processes, and fostering empowerment, educators are better equipped to engage in transformative learning experiences themselves and, in turn, create similar opportunities for their students. This approach not only enhances teaching practices but also cultivates a culture of continuous growth and development within the academic community.

STRATEGIES FOR FOSTERING EQUITY AND ANTI-RACISM

As the director for the Center for Teaching Excellence, being a Latina woman in higher education leadership has significantly impacted my professional journey and personal growth. My intersectional identity as both an educator and a member of a historically marginalized group has shaped my perspective and approach within the field of adult education. One of the key impacts of my identity as a Latina woman in a leadership role is the firsthand experience I have had in navigating the challenges posed by systemic inequities. These challenges include facing implicit biases in the workplace, encountering limited representation of diverse voices in leadership positions, and dealing with cultural assumptions about the capabilities and contributions of women and people of color. These experiences have not only influenced my leadership style but have also fueled my commitment to promoting DEI within the Center for Teaching Excellence. As a Latina woman in higher education leadership, I have been able to bring a unique perspective to the table. My lived experiences have allowed me to better understand the needs and experiences of underrepresented groups within the academic community. This understanding has informed the development of programs and initiatives within the CTE that aim to support and empower educators from diverse backgrounds. Furthermore, my identity as a Latina woman in a leadership role has served as a source of inspiration for others within the academic community. By breaking barriers and challenging stereotypes, I have been able to serve as a role model for aspiring leaders from similar backgrounds. This representation is crucial in fostering a more inclusive and equitable environment within higher education. In conclusion, being a Latina woman in higher education leadership has had a profound impact on my professional journey, shaping my perspective, leadership style, and commitment to diversity and inclusion within the Center for Teaching Excellence. My experiences have not only enriched my own growth but have also contributed to creating a more inclusive and supportive environment for educators from all backgrounds.

In the pursuit of fostering DEIA within adult education, creating learning environments where all individuals feel seen, heard, and valued is paramount. This can be exemplified through various practices and initiatives that aim to promote inclusivity and combat biases. One example of creating a culture where individuals feel seen, heard, and valued is through the implementation of diverse representation in educational materials. This can include using textbooks, readings, and multimedia resources that showcase a wide range of perspectives and voices from different backgrounds. By incorporating diverse content, learners are exposed to a variety of experiences and viewpoints, which can help validate their own identities and promote a sense of belonging. Another example is the establishment of safe spaces for open dialogue and discussion. Providing opportunities for students to share their thoughts, experiences, and concerns in a respectful and supportive environment can help ensure that their voices are heard and valued. Facilitating conversations around sensitive topics such as race, gender, and privilege can also encourage critical reflection and challenge harmful biases among learners.

My background drives me to develop inclusive pedagogy, provide mentorship to learners and faculty from marginalized groups, and contribute to research focused on creating a more equitable and just educational landscape. My professional trajectory and scholarly pursuits have profoundly influenced my commitment to cultivating inclusive pedagogical practices, offering guidance and support to students and educators hailing from underrepresented communities, and engaging in scholarly investigations aimed at fostering a fairer and more egalitarian educational environment. My personal journey, marked by experiences that have underscored the significance of diversity and inclusivity in education, has been instrumental in shaping my dedication to advancing inclusive pedagogy. Through encounters with individuals from diverse backgrounds and exposure to the challenges faced by marginalized groups within educational settings, I have come to recognize the imperative of adopting pedagogical approaches that cater to the needs and perspectives of all learners. This recognition has fueled my passion for developing inclusive teaching strategies that not only acknowledge the diversity of student populations but also actively work toward dismantling barriers to learning and success. Moreover, my interactions with learners and faculty members from marginalized communities have underscored the importance of mentorship and support in fostering academic and professional growth. Witnessing firsthand the transformative impact of mentorship on individuals facing systemic barriers has reinforced my belief in the power of mentorship to empower and uplift marginalized voices within academia. By providing mentorship to individuals from underrepresented groups, I aim to contribute to the creation of a more inclusive and supportive educational environment where all individuals have the opportunity to thrive and succeed. Furthermore, my scholarly endeavors are driven by a deep-seated commitment to advancing social justice and equity within the realm of education. Through research initiatives focused on promoting inclusivity, diversity, and equity in educational practices, I seek to generate knowledge that can inform policy and practice, ultimately working toward a more just and equitable educational landscape for all. By engaging in research that addresses the systemic inequalities present in education, I strive to contribute meaningfully to the ongoing efforts to create a more inclusive and equitable educational system that values and uplifts every individual.

CONTRIBUTIONS OF STUDENTS

Students engaging in self-reflection to uncover biases and assumptions play a pivotal role in fostering equity and anti-racism in adult education (Ashforth et al., 2008). By participating in cross-cultural exchanges and exploring diverse perspectives, students enhance their cultural competency, a crucial step toward creating an inclusive learning environment.

EMPOWERING FACULTY

Faculty members are key drivers of change in adult education. Continuous professional development focusing on inclusive pedagogy, anti-racism practices, and culturally responsive teaching equips them with essential skills (Ashforth et al., 2008). Moreover, revisiting curriculum content for inclusivity and establishing peer mentorship programs further strengthens faculty efforts in promoting diversity and equity.

SUPPORTING STAFF

Creating an inclusive environment in adult education involves equipping staff with cultural competency training and promoting equitable hiring practices (Ashforth et al., 2008). Providing spaces for staff from diverse backgrounds to share experiences and address equity concerns fosters a sense of belonging and support within the institution.

INSTITUTIONAL COMMITMENT

Administrators play a crucial role in setting the tone for institutional commitment to DEI. By articulating a clear vision, allocating resources, and analyzing student success data, administrators can identify achievement gaps and implement targeted interventions (Ashforth et al., 2008). Additionally, policymakers advocating for legislation promoting equitable access and funding parity contribute significantly to systemic change in adult education.

Achieving equity and promoting anti-racism in the realm of adult education is an ongoing process that necessitates unwavering dedication, cooperative efforts, and introspection at every echelon of the educational framework. Through the adoption of these methodologies, stakeholders within the adult education sector can collectively strive toward establishing inclusive and equitable learning environments that uphold principles of justice for all individuals involved.

REFERENCES

Ashforth, B., Harrison, S., & Corley, K. (2008). Identification in organizations: An examination of four fundamental questions. *Journal of Management, 34*(3), 325–374. https://doi.org/10.1177/0149206308316059

Cranton, P. (1994). *Understanding and promoting transformative learning: A guide for educators of adults.* Jossey-Bass.

Mezirow, J. (1997). Transformative learning theory to practice. *New Directions for Adult and Continuing Education, 74,* 5–12.

ADDITIONAL READINGS

DeBombari, V., Lopez, R. D. G., & Hernandez, M. E. (2019). Transformative learning for equity and social justice in higher education. *Journal of College Student Development, 60*(2), 223–242.

Mezirow, J. (2000). *Learning to think like an adult: Contemporary principles of developmental education* (2nd ed.). Jossey-Bass.

CHAPTER 3

EMPOWERING ADULT LEARNERS THROUGH CASE-BASED INSTRUCTION: A NEW APPROACH TO EMPLOYABILITY SKILLS

Alexis Guethler
University of Maryland Baltimore, USA

Sharon Ultsch
Education Developer and Independent Researcher, USA

ABSTRACT

Case-based instruction (CBI), commonly used in fields such as law, business, and medicine, is less prevalent in adult education and workforce development. This article examines the implementation of CBI in an employability skills orientation course within a workforce training program. As a problem-based instructional strategy, CBI supports the development of transferable soft skills, such as effective communication, by promoting inquiry, problem-solving, and discovery. It engages adult learners in collaborative, meaningful learning and encourages the integration of their life experiences. Grounded in constructivist learning theory, the article aligns CBI with the four stages of Kolb's experiential learning cycle: concrete experience, reflective observation, abstract conceptualization, and active experimentation. Instructional strategies mapped to each stage are provided to guide practitioners in applying CBI effectively. The article also highlights the value of authentic, profession-specific cases developed in collaboration with subject matter experts to immerse learners in realistic work scenarios. By situating learners in real-life contexts, CBI enables reflection and application of employability skills relevant to their professions. This approach fosters professional competence while connecting learners to the sociocultural dimensions of their chosen career paths

Keywords: Case-based instruction (CBI); workforce development; experiential learning; employability skills; adult education

Workforce development programs aim to blend technical career training with workplace social and professional skills, commonly known as "employability skills," such as communication, dependability, and customer service. However, vocational education has not adequately addressed the growing need for these skills (Burner et al., 2019), leaving entry-level learners lacking the sociocultural knowledge crucial for success (Smith et al., 2019). Instructional strategies designed for adult learners are needed to bridge the gap between training and succeeding in new careers.

Prevailing definitions of employability skills often reflect a narrow cultural framework that prioritizes productivity, conformity, and self-reliance as hallmarks of professionalism. While these traits may be valuable, treating them as universal can perpetuate bias, overlook strengths in other cultures, and pressure students to code-switch to fit dominant norms. Critical theorists, including Townsend (2006), argue that adult education often upholds the capitalist class system by normalizing whiteness in workplace behavior standards. In contrast to this dominant narrative, they advocate for employing training opportunities to foster critical consciousness in participants, challenging the dominant influence in our work culture. While promoting a critical perspective on workplace practices is essential for transformation, equipping learners with an understanding of prevailing employer expectations is equally critical. This dual approach, which is often in tension, empowers them to navigate these norms thoughtfully, granting them the agency to make informed decisions about their behavior and identity at work. Without including a critical lens, we risk either reinforcing existing biases or leaving workers ill-equipped to confront professional realities, undermining their potential to drive meaningful change in their lives and workplaces.

This chapter explores the use of case-based instruction (CBI) as an innovative approach to teaching employability skills grounded in the principles of adult learning theory. Rooted in adult learning theory, this chapter explores how CBI, when developed and used critically, can address the unique challenges and constraints of teaching employability skills.

As aspiring anti-racist educators, Alexis Guethler and Sharon Ultsch sought to use CBI to confront the ethical challenge of developing an employability skills program which would make transparent workplace expectations often shaped by dominant white American culture without compromising learners' authenticity and lived experiences, a design conundrum. By engaging learners in realistic scenarios and encouraging them to draw upon and share their diverse experiences, CBI cultivated a deeper and hopefully more critical perspective as well as a more personal understanding of employability skills. Alexis, an instructional designer, crafted the curriculum. Later, Sharon, a critical pedagogue, applied a critical evaluation lens with the goal of suggesting methods by which we could adapt the curriculum and faculty training in ways that empower learners to challenge assumptions and advocate for more equitable and inclusive workplaces.

Throughout this chapter, and especially in the following coda, we will share why and how we used CBI and how our collaborative review of the curriculum suggested new ways to empower our learners. First, we examine the pedagogical challenges of employability skills training, the theoretical underpinnings of CBI rooted in adult learning principles, and how CBI was implemented in our workforce training program. Next, we offer practical suggestions for creating inclusive case materials. Finally, we bring readers along with us on our praxis journey as we strive to be reflexive of our own practices and educational artifacts to advance social justice.

THE AUTHORS AND OUR COURSE DEVELOPMENT TEAM

To ensure learners were prepared for success in their future employment, the workforce training division of our local community college commissioned a unique curriculum intertwining employability skills with existing training in job interviewing and resume writing. Despite employee technical competence, employer feedback indicated a gap in employability skills among our newly trained graduates, echoing findings reflected in the literature (Cukier et al., 2015; Smith et al., 2019). Our training program needed to support career changers, emergent bilingual adults, and GED program graduates transitioning to skilled training with the explicit aim to rapidly advance adults into family-sustaining careers.

In this chapter, I, Alexis, will share how I employed CBI as a method of honoring the needs and experiences of adult learners. At the time, I was working as an instructional designer tasked with content development and faculty training for this program as part of a workforce development unit at a community college. I hold a PhD. in instructional technology focusing on online course design. This project challenged me to use that expertise to develop a synchronous online course to equip adult learners with the essential social capital and skills for workforce success. Developing an employability skills program also presented a dilemma for me as a white woman without direct experience in the building, technical, and healthcare trades that learners would be studying. Finding a single subject matter expert would have been impractical for this project. Therefore, I relied on a team of educators and career coaches familiar with our students and the culturally defined norms they were expected to understand in our local job market. Our career success coaches, employer advisory board, and adjunct faculty practitioners provided invaluable insights from the fields into which they hire our students, helping to bridge the gap between academic preparation and real-world expectations. Their input was critical in ensuring that our curriculum was not just theoretically sound but practically relevant. Our career coaches walk side by side with our students from recruitment to job placement and, therefore, understand the career challenges our students face in fields that may not value their individual experiences and identities. As Black and Latino women, the success coaches acted as "critical readers," helping me identify my own normative assumptions. This process of self-reflection and critique was uncomfortable at times, but it was essential for my growth as an educator and the development of a truly inclusive curriculum.

I, Sharon, joined the team after the initial curriculum development phase while Alexis was piloting the employability skills course. I am an instructional designer who also brought to this project extensive experience as an adult educator, professor, and faculty developer working with a diverse group of learners and educators. My doctorate in Educational Policy & Leadership focuses on Critical Pedagogy and Institutional Ethnography, which has deeply informed my approach to curriculum development and educational practice. In my work, I advocate for the importance of using a critical lens to interrogate the prevailing dominant story, in this case, 'employability skills.' While Alexis' initial focus in this curriculum was to avoid perpetuating biases—an important first step. I saw an opportunity for us to create something more transformative together. My goal was to assist Alexis in developing a curriculum that would empower both students and faculty to identify and name systems of oppression in education and the workplace. We want to encourage them, in the Freirean tradition, to critically read their world (Freire, 1985) through interrogating case studies, engaging in dialogue and applying self-reflection. In this chapter, you'll hear my voice most clearly in our discussions of ongoing reflexive praxis. This process of continuous reflection and refinement of our practices has been central to our collaborative design approach, allowing us to critically examine our own assumptions and biases as we continue to develop different curricula for adult learners.

LEVERAGING ADULT LEARNING PRINCIPLES FOR WORKFORCE EMPOWERMENT

Storytelling is a powerful tool for addressing the complexities of social systems and skills (Boffo, 2020). Stories invite us to step into the role of another person, imagining different perspectives. In the Freirean tradition, storytelling is a powerful way to counter dominant narratives that perpetuate negative stereotypes and images that harm marginalized groups (Ishimaru et al., 2023). Storytelling holds particular promise for adult learners seeking to understand the socio-cultural knowledge and skills required in their future professions as they make sense of the historical moment in which they live (Machado, 2023). Storytelling in pedagogy theory goes by many names: scenario-based learning, narrative pedagogy, CBI, or, in military contexts, 'sea stories.' This chapter will use the term CBI (Kolodner et al., 2012). CBI combines storytelling with prompts that ask students to discuss, reflect, and adapt definitions of core workplace skills to include their experiences and identities. This approach is crucial because it allows students to critically engage with case studies by discussing the point of view of the employee, coworkers, customers, and supervisors to develop a more holistic view of how employability skills impact real-world scenarios. Moreover, a story-centric approach like CBI invites students into the learning process, fostering their understanding of institutional systems by encouraging them to critically examine various aspects of institutional life, including the workplace. By reflecting on their own experiences and comparing them with fictional situations, students have the opportunity to interpret and learn from their past, ultimately enhancing their ability to navigate future career challenges and, as mentioned earlier, read the world by discerning biases and power relations in political and social life.

Andragogy presents an operational framework of assumptions and correlated instructional principles to describe the needs of adult students (Knowles et al., 2015). This framework incorporates strategies that serve adult learners by applying them to their careers and life roles through experiential learning activities. We elaborate briefly on the andragogy assumptions most relevant to this discussion: adults want to *apply* what they learn directly to their world and learn most effectively through *problem-solving*. The literature recommends that learning experiences be well-structured, practical, and collaborative so that students have the best learning outcomes (Carlson et al., 2018). Adults want to experience rather than listen to content; they use what they learn, apply it to their lives, and work to find solutions to new problems (Knowles et al., 2015). This relevancy and applicability motivate the adult learner (Chen, 2014).

Relevancy is also a central principle in critical pedagogy as it humanizes the classroom. Our adult students bring diverse backgrounds, prior learning experiences, and knowledge into the classroom; therefore, course designs that highlight and include this diversity create opportunities for learners to reflect on and interact with the material that is culturally relevant to students' past experiences and future goals.

Problem-solving fosters big-picture thinking; it is experiential and inquiry-based compared to the content-orientation of traditional pedagogy. CBI is a problem-based approach in which learners must recall old experiences, interpret the new situation, and adapt an older solution to meet the new problem posed by the case (Knowles et al., 2015). Problem-posing, a foundational concept in critical pedagogy, recognizes that knowledge is not deposited from the teacher to the student but is formulated in dialogue between the two. Adult learners bring abundant information sources to fuel such problem-based inquiry, and they simultaneously appreciate the opportunity to solve problems relevant to their future careers (Knowles et al., 2015). Thus, instruction that focuses on developing new strategies to solve realistic cases matches the needs and interests of adult learners and is likely to improve motivation and learning outcomes.

CASE-BASED INSTRUCTION IN PRACTICE

We employed CBI to encourage adult learners to use their lived experiences to adapt standardized employability skills definitions drawn from the US Department of Labor's SCANS (ACT Inc, 2000) competencies as well as the National Network of Business and Industry Associations' training frameworks. We believe students need to connect employability skills to their existing knowledge and experiences to gain the full benefits of workforce training. Lyon and Bandura (2020) suggest that CBI initiates learners into a profession's sociocultural knowledge by practicing critical thinking with authentic problems. CBI helps learners apply their knowledge and experiences to new scenarios, enhancing their professional skills relevant to future employment (Cukier et al., 2015; Lyons & Bandura, 2020). When engaging with contextualized case studies (stories adapted from real-life scenarios) learners are encouraged to predict how they would perceive the case based on various roles, such as employer, supervisor, and customer. These shifts in perspective foster the exploration of ideas, integrating learners' personal experiences with theoretical knowledge (Knowles, 2015). Further, students gain vicarious experience by confronting realistic situations, predicting the best course of action, and comparing their judgments with those of other students.

The cases were tailored to skilled trades, healthcare, and technical helpdesk, letting learners explore skills relevant to their careers. Our instructional approach unfolds in four critical phases: a content module that provides a foundational definition and positive case of the skill in action, asynchronous online discussions of a second case scenario for initial engagement, synchronous class discussions for deeper exploration, and a reflective journal in which learners recorded their new understandings. We used a dual case strategy which allowed for contrasting examples and diverse character representation based on real people. These narratives showcased the practical application of skills alongside the standard skill definitions, illustrating the tangible benefits for employers and employees.

We then presented cases with problems requiring resolution, prompting students to apply reasoning and adapt skill definitions. CBI's strength is turning ill-structured problems without clear answers into opportunities for problem-solving and analytical thinking practice (Kolodner et al., 2012). This fostered critical engagement and deeper understanding of skills' real-world applicability. Through online forums, learners independently identified issues in case studies using their experiences, preparing for peer discussions.

Next, career development instructors facilitated synchronous conversations allowing students from varied cultural backgrounds to collaboratively challenge and expand upon their judgments. The act of analyzing cases provides practical experience in problem-solving and reinforces the judgment necessary to demonstrate employability skills. These cases are purposefully ambiguous and require learners to grapple with what is known, unknown, or assumed. During these synchronous sessions, the instructor highlights student-suggested interventions that promise positive outcomes or reveal underlying issues in the cases. Students collectively redefine these competencies by integrating their lived experiences, fostering a deeper comprehension that transcends traditional definitions. In their exit survey, one student stated, "Case study discussions really enabled you to consider different situations in a third person perspective. This removes a biased opinion when you're involved, allowing you to consider how you would handle the situation in a professional manner."

Finally, students submit an independent reflection on the case study. They are asked to discuss similar experiences in their own lives. Students contemplate alternative outcomes informed by their newly acquired understanding of essential employability skills by drawing on personal experiences from previous jobs, education, or family roles. A student's course evaluation illustrates this transformation:

> Before taking this class, I tried to do my best, but I was not sure what was the right way. During this class, I understood what kind of skills I need and how I can use them in the workplace.

Helyer (2015) underscores the importance of reflection in developing transferable knowledge, emphasizing how such introspection can guide learners in reimagining past situations with a fresh perspective.

Reflecting on case studies directly engages with the adult learners' motivations, connecting prior experience to new learning and applying concepts to immediate goals, such as job seeking.

Our application of CBI, informed by adult learning theory, emphasizes practicality and collaboration, as recommended by contemporary research on adult education (Merriam & Bierema, 2014). In hindsight, it also supports a critical pedagogical approach by incorporating active learning with dialogue and self-reflection. By structuring learning activities that promote collaboration among learners from diverse backgrounds, we not only support the adult learners' preference for social learning but also enhance their ability to work within diverse teams, a critical employability skill in today's globalized workforce. This methodology not only cultivates a comprehensive understanding of employability skills but also empowers students to make informed choices in their professional lives. They learn to navigate workplace norms reflectively, enabling them to actively balance employer expectations with their values and identity. Our hope in this design was that this learning experience would foster a more nuanced understanding of the complexities of workplace relationships. Additionally, we wanted to illuminate and unveil what might be hidden expectations of the dominant cultural group that are not apparent to our students from diverse cultural backgrounds.

CREATING INCLUSIVE CASE-STUDY MATERIALS

Creating new, relevant case materials for employee workplace settings required skillful storytelling and significant time investment. Developing practical, ambiguous, real-world scenarios with multiple "correct" answers was essential to promote argumentation guided by employer stakeholders for authenticity (Jonassen & Hernandez-Serrano, 2002; Samkin & Keevy, 2019). Existing employability curricula, tailored for high school students, appeared potentially patronizing to older adults, leading to the development of custom case libraries, a significant time commitment.

As the assigned instructional designer, I, Alexis, recognized that I was not an expert in employability skills. To develop cases that were contextualized to each of our employment pathways, I began with an extensive review of industry articles and trade journals, in addition to spending time with practitioners in each field. I relied on interviews, focus groups, and member-checking with instructors, employers, and an advisory council to gather specific details I would craft into cases. In each situation, I had to take into account how each contributor's biases, emotion, and knowledge of real people beyond the stories influenced their accounts. I typically synthesized multiple similar accounts into case studies representing authentic scenarios with nuanced challenges and solutions. However, it was also important to me not to replicate existing stereotypes within the stories as they were told to me. CBI is only an anti-racist pedagogy when we avoid evoking and reinforcing stereotypes.

We offer the following suggestions that we used to develop these cases and, more recently, to revise cases for more inclusive language:

- Include a critical editor or peer in the writing process. All writers have biases, many of which we are unaware. Find another DEI-minded individual with whom you can partner to act as a second reader about your products.
- Use a DEI curriculum assessment checklist or tool as a guideline for developing inclusive cases, expanding awareness of inclusive practices, and providing a self-assessment tool. Recommended resources:
  - The Inclusive & Bias-Free Curriculum Checklist is an interactive tool designed to assess case study materials, including representation across many factors (University of Nebraska Medical Center, n.d, adapted from Caruso et al., 2019).
  - The Washington Model Resource: Screening for Biased Content in Instructional Materials is a downloadable checklist for large curriculum review projects such as course or textbook reviews (Washington Office of Superintendent of Public Instruction, 2021).
- Represent diverse identities respectfully. When basing a positive story on a real person, describe them to the extent their identity is known and permitted. Avoid assigning names commonly associated with specific racial or ethnic identities to characters involved in negative behaviors, as this can unintentionally perpetuate harmful stereotypes (Crabtree et al., 2023). Careful selection of names promotes inclusivity and prevents introduction of biases into cases. The following sources can be used to determine character names:
  - Crabtree et al. (2023) provide open access to a database of 600 names along with the assumptions most often associated with each name for use by researchers and curriculum designers.
  - Popular name selection sites now offer gender-neutral categories, which are valuable for avoiding traditional gender roles in case studies.
- It is not always possible to have content reviewed by human reviewers. Large Language Model tools like generative AI can be employed when human reviewers are not available. While acknowledging that AI tools can perpetuate systematic biases derived from public training materials, these tools are also highly effective at

identifying stereotypes in materials provided to them. Checking your work can also help you reflect on your biases and improve inclusive language use and storytelling over time. The following prompt is a good way to start:
- I need assistance in identifying any stereotypes, biases, or non-inclusive language in a story I've written. As an editor prioritizing inclusivity and aiming to eliminate micro-aggressions, please help me recognize and rephrase problematic elements to create a more sensitive and inclusive narrative.

Our curriculum did not initially contain resources designed to "train the trainer." However, during interviews with instructors, they noted that CBI discussions presented challenges in ensuring that learners did not default to stereotypes, indicating a need for strategies to disrupt and redirect in a teachable way, sometimes called micro-interventions. Recognizing the importance of preparing faculty to facilitate critical discussions, I sought guidance from Sharon to better understand the professional development needs of the instructors tasked with leading CBI sessions. This collaboration highlighted the need to support faculty in identifying and addressing microaggressions that could arise from learner biases and in fostering an environment that encourages sensitivity to cultural differences.

In preparing to teach others about our curriculum, Sharon and I had the opportunity to engage in reflexive praxis, examining our assumptions, the curriculum itself, the faculty's role, and ways we might join with them to promote critical consciousness among students. The initial design aimed to foster positive representation and minimize harm. In our ongoing collegial critical dialogues, I recognized that the curriculum fell short of challenging normative values and deficit perspectives. This led to the sometimes-uncomfortable process of re-evaluating my own work, and I was grateful to have Sharon's critical lens as we collaboratively learned through this curriculum evaluation. By sharing a coda below in which Sharon reflects on possible curriculum revisions, we aim to demonstrate the ongoing process of challenging and interrogating our work as we move toward becoming more critical and culturally responsive practitioners. We also wanted to support others in utilizing CBI with even more skill and critical awareness than we had achieved in this first project.

CODA: OUR PROCESS OF REFLEXIVE PRAXIS

In co-reflecting on our work, we came to believe that this curriculum unintentionally replicated harmful norms by failing to encourage learners to challenge assumptions of "normative" behaviors embedded in employability skills definitions. Guided by Freire (1993) and other critical pedagogues, we examined our habitual thinking, relationship to this work, and roles in designing such curricula within the neoliberal higher education context. We questioned whether our curriculum truly challenged implicit biases or merely served as "window dressing." We asked: How might we foster inclusive thinking that challenges oppressive systems in our students and faculty?

Prompting critical consciousness is the first step in implementing a Freirean model of pedagogy, that seeks to empower students by encouraging them to bring their lived experiences into the classroom. This approach encourages adult learners to go beyond existing beliefs and critically examine their lived experiences as socially constructed. In our discussions, we understood that faculty teaching a case-based curriculum must model and promote this critical consciousness by teaching students to evaluate their own needs, experiences, and reasons for learning the material in a broader social-political context. This process involves asking fundamental questions, such as: Why are these specific skills emphasized? Who benefits from this curriculum design? Are other important skills being overlooked, and if so, why? And how does this curriculum perpetuate or challenge systemic biases?

Moreover, we realized there is power in naming and challenging the deficit model that often underpins employability skills curricula, where certain groups of learners are viewed as needing to be "fixed." This deficit perspective also revealed a "hidden curriculum" that tends to benefit some groups over others. By asking faculty to lead students in questioning and naming the systems around them, we aim to help learners better understand social capital, privilege, and power operating in the workplace. We hope we have enabled them to use this awareness to gain experience and, ultimately, to improve their fields from within.

Having problematized our curriculum through this reflexive praxis, we would like to acknowledge the partnership required between instructional faculty and designers to bring critical pedagogies to life. In our discussion, we asked ourselves how we, as instructional designers, could best prepare curricula in which faculty would become co-learners with the students that the curriculum is designed to teach. We believe that we could begin this process by being transparent about our own hopes and reservations for this curriculum, empowering faculty to engage with us in an ongoing dialog about what we mean when we define "employability skills." In addition, we would reframe our instructor materials to highlight the goal of using CBI to create spaces for critical dialogue rather than achieving agreement on definitions and skills through class discussion.

Moreover, we would adapt our student and faculty resource prompts to focus on problem-posing rather than problem-solving. Such prompts challenge learners to scrutinize the broader social and political contexts in which these case studies occur. Questions might include: What systemic factors contribute to the situations presented? How do social capital and workplace norms create barriers to advancement for some groups? What assumptions underpin the proposed solutions, and who benefits from them? Such questioning promotes critical consciousness, urging learners to examine the origins, omissions, and implications of what they know or think they know about a case. Ultimately, this problem-posing approach aims to cultivate a critical perspective that goes beyond simply recognizing social context and moves toward advocacy or intervention. It lays the groundwork for challenging traditional hierarchies and empowers learners to take action, promoting equity and fostering a more transformative educational experience.

CONCLUSION

In this chapter, we explored the potential of CBI as an effective method for teaching employability skills to adult learners. As instructional designers and educators, we focused on creating educational experiences that are practical, skill-oriented, inclusive, and reflective of diverse lived experiences. In this process, however, we questioned this work's underlying social and cultural benefits. It is true that CBI allows adult learners to engage with real-world scenarios and provides a rich learning environment where they can apply their existing knowledge and skills. However, in the broader context of vocational training, we recognize that instructional designers can also be complicit in replicating dominant norms, hierarchies, and beliefs. CBI has the potential to encourage critical consciousness-raising, but we believe we have to intentionally design for it, train instructors to foster dialogue, and promote critical analysis that encourages empowerment and agency in learners.

With the affordances of CBI for adult learners in mind, we offer recommendations to aid practitioners, administrators, and scholars in considering this constructivist instructional approach. By grounding our curriculum in adult learning theory while weaving in inclusive and antiracist pedagogies, we prepare learners for the practical realities of the workplace and the challenges of working in and contributing to a diverse and equitable society. Through critical dialogue and re-examining our curriculum, we identified areas where our approach could be strengthened to avoid perpetuating the deficit model and systemic biases. The coda represents our commitment to foster a more inclusive educational environment by inviting faculty and learners to engage in deeper questioning, exploring hidden biases, and promoting a problem-posing approach to learning. By integrating strategies that encourage reflection, challenge systemic inequities, and cultivate a broader perspective, we aim to create a curriculum that not only equips learners with essential skills but also inspires them to question and transform the systems in which they work.

REFERENCES

ACT Inc. (2000). Workplace essential skills: Resources related to the SCANS competencies and foundation skills. https://www.dol.gov/sites/dolgov/files/ETA/publications/00-wes.pdf

Boffo, V. (2020). Storytelling and other skills: Building employability in higher education. In R. Egetenmeyer, V. Boffo, & S. Kröner (Eds.), *International and comparative studies in adult and continuing education* (pp. 31–50). Firenze University Press. https://doi.org/10.36253/978-88-5518-155-6.03

Burner, T., Supinski, L., Zhu, S., Robinson, S., & Supinski, C. (2019). *The global skills shortage: Bridging the talent gap with education, training, and sourcing.* Society for Human Resource Management. https://www.shrm.org/content/dam/en/shrm/topics-tools/news/employee-relations/SHRM-Skills-Gap-2019.pdf. Accessed on July 2, 2024.

Carlson, R., Padron, K., & Andrews, C. (2018). Evidence-based instructional strategies for adult learners: A review of the literature. *Codex, 4*(4), 29–47.

Caruso, A. B., Hobart, T. R., Botash, A. S., & Germain, L. J. (2019). Can a checklist ameliorate implicit bias in medical education?. *Medical Education, 53*(5), 510. https://europepmc.org/article/med/30856280

Chen, J. C. (2014). Teaching nontraditional adult students: Adult learning theories in practice. *Teaching in Higher Education, 19*(4), 406–418. https://doi.org/10.1080/13562517.2013.860101

Crabtree, C., Kim, J. Y., Gaddis, S. M., Holbein, J. B., Guage, C., & Marx, W. W. (2023). Validated names for experimental studies on race and ethnicity. *Scientific Data, 10*(1), 130. https://doi.org/10.17605/OSF.IO/AHPVQ

Cukier, W., Hodson, J., & Omar, A. (2015). *"Soft" skills are hard: A review of the literature.* Social Sciences and Humanities Research Council. https://www.ryerson.ca/diversity/reports/soft-skills-are-hard-a-review-of-the-literature/

Freire, P. (1985). Reading the world and reading the word: An interview with Paulo Freire. *Language Arts, 62*(1), 15–21. http://www.jstor.org/stable/41405241

Freire, P. (1993). *Pedagogy of the oppressed* New rev (20th-Anniversary ed.). Continuum.

Helyer, R. (2015). Learning through reflection: The critical role of reflection in work-based learning. *Journal of Work-Applied Management, 7*(1), 15–27. https://doi.org/10.1108/jwam-10-2015-003

Ishimaru, A. M., Craig, A. B., Daw, C. E., & Jackson, W. (2023). Through the pandemic portal: Turning to community to cultivate a relational paradigm of leadership. *VUE (Voices in Urban Education), 51*(1). https://doi.org/10.35240/vue.28

Jonassen, D. H., & Hernandez-Serrano, J. (2002). Case-based reasoning and instructional design: Using stories to problem solving. *Educational Technology Research & Development, 50*(2), 65–77. https://doi.org/10.1007/BF02504994

Knowles, M., Holton III, E. F., & Swanson, R. A. (2015). *The adult learner* (8th ed.). Routledge.

Kolodner, J. L., Dorn, B., Thomas, J. O., & Guzdial, M. (2012). Theory of practice of case-based learning aids. In D. H. Jonassen & S. Land (Eds.), *Theoretical foundations of learning environments* (2nd ed., pp. 142–170). Routledge.

Lyons, P., & Bandura, R. P. (2020). Skills needs, integrative pedagogy, and case-based instruction. *Journal of Workplace Learning*, *32*(7), 473–487. https://doi.org/10.1108/JWL-12-2019-0140

Machado, M. (2023). Family stories matter: Critical pedagogy of storytelling in elementary classrooms. *VUE (Voices in Urban Education)*, *51*(1). https://doi.org/10.35240/vue.26

Merriam, S. B., & Bierema, L. L. (2014). *Adult learning: Linking theory and practice* (1st ed.). Jossey-Bass.

National Network of Business and Industry Associations. (2014). *Common employability skills: A foundation for success in the workplace*. https://www.necessaryskillsnow.org/employability-skills.php. Accessed on January 15, 2022.

Samkin, G., & Keevy, M. (2019). Using a stakeholder developed case study to develop soft skills. *Meditari Accountancy Research*, *27*(6), 862–882. https://doi.org/10.1108/MEDAR-01-2018-0260

Smith, E., Tsin, D., & Rogers, E. (2019). Who will succeed in tomorrow's job market? Bridging the soft skills gap for a more equitable talent pipeline. Urban Alliance. https://theurbanalliance.org/wp-content/uploads/2019/10/UA_WP2019_Who_Will_Succeed_in_Tomorrows_Job_Market.pdf

Townsend, R. (2006). Adult, community, and public education as primary sites for the development of social capital. *Australian Journal of Adult Learning*, *46*(2), 153–174.

University of Nebraska Medical Center. (n.d.). *Bias-free curriculum checklist*. https://www.unmc.edu/facdev/resources/diversity-resources/bias-checklist.html. Accessed on April 11, 2024.

Washington Office of Superintendent of Public Instruction. (2021). Screening for biased content in instructional materials (Version 1.2). *OSPI*. https://ospi.k12.wa.us/sites/default/files/2022-12/WA-ScreeningForBiasedContent.pdf. Accessed on April 11, 2024.

SECTION 2

SUPPORTING DIVERSE LEARNERS AND PEDAGOGICAL INNOVATION

CHAPTER 4

FIRST-GEN, SECOND CHANCE: IDENTIFYING AND SUPPORTING FIRST-GEN ADULT LEARNERS[1]

La'Tonya "LT" Rease Miles
Education Developer and Santa Clara University, USA

ABSTRACT

This chapter focuses on the intersection of adult learners and first-generation college students. Using a strengths-based approach, it will describe the unique characteristics of this population and will offer specific recommendations for how practitioners may support these students. According to a 2023 NASPA report, over 30% of first-generation students are age 30 or over yet there is little scholarship about their experiences. This essay will provide a foundation for others to build upon.

Keywords: Adult learners; first-generation college students; higher education; student support strategies; strengths-based approach

My mother and I hold the unique distinction of being "first-generation college graduates," as the term is commonly defined.[2] Mom, a single parent, enlisted in the military to provide a better life for us and for her to be able to afford college specifically. I was a year old at her high school graduation.

At age 10, I recall sitting on the edge of her bed and taking a deep sniff of her business marketing textbook for a course that she was taking at Midlands Technical College in Columbia, South Carolina. Mom swirled in and out of community college (Bahr, 2012; Katsinas et al., 2019) and, almost 20 years later, with the help of credit for prior learning (Klein-Collins & Framularo, 2022), she earned a bachelor's degree three years after me.

"Taking classes" as opposed to going to college was the norm in my family. In addition to Mom, my grandmother enrolled in a few evening classes; my older cousin accidentally earned an A.A. just by being an off and on part-time student over several years; and even one of my uncles earned a degree while doing time. These so-called nontraditional pathways were commonplace, and my matriculation at a four-year school was the outlier higher education experience. As a result, I was attuned to what I would later learn was "adult education" because it was normalized in my family.

I solemnly promised that if I ever became a college president, it would be at a school like Mom's alma mater, Trinity College in Washington, D.C., whose adult learner population at the time primarily were Black women (Schmalz, 2015). Although I have yet to become a college president, I have made good on my promise to affirm and to validate the first-gen and nontraditional student as a former Dean of Student Affairs at a small private college; as a consultant for community colleges and four-year institutions nationally; as a founder of a media advocacy organization dedicated to transfer, adult learner, and first-gen experiences; as a faculty member in a graduate program with a critical mass of returning students; and as a subject matter expert for an organization dedicated to the re-engagement and re-enrollment of adult learners, many of whom are first-generation to college. Adult education is not just business for me; it is personal.

SPEAK TO HOW YOUR WORK OR RESEARCH RELATES TO DIVERSITY, EQUITY, INCLUSION, AND ANTI-RACISM (DEIA) WITHIN THE CONTEXTS OF ADULT EDUCATION

Currently, I work as a campus liaison and subject matter expert for ReUp Education, an organization that is dedicated solely to adult learners, specifically those like my mother, my husband, and me who started college but had to pause our education for a host of reasons: running out of money, having children, taking care of others, getting stationed someplace else, life. As of this writing, there are over 40 million Americans who fall in this category, i.e., having some credits but no credential or degree (National Student Clearinghouse Research Center, 2023). Notably, a critical mass of these individuals are people of color, especially Black and Latinx, working-class, rural residents, undocumented, and first-generation to college

(2023). These stopouts, or non-completers, often are tracked and trapped into low wage jobs with little room for upward mobility. As a result, they are systematically disadvantaged and under-resourced.

To convince Institutions of Higher Education (IHEs) that the rewards are worth the low return on investment to reach the stopout population,[3] at ReUp we highlight the adult learner's ecosystem, including their family life, employment situation, and overall well-being, and we centralize their narratives. Rodriguez (2024) puts things in plain terms: "Storytelling is a potent means of cultivating empathy, understanding, and meaningful change." Regarding the narratives of first-generation students particularly, she argues that storytelling, as opposed to just raw data like re-enrollment, retention, or graduation rates, (a) makes first-gen experiences more relatable; (b) may inspire educators and policymakers to implement change; and (c) provide venues or spaces for student community building while fostering resiliency and sense of belonging.

Although the so-called demographic cliff looms over higher education, many enrollment managers remain focused on the traditional direct from high school population to meet their enrollment or retention goals. Meanwhile, the adult learner population continues to be overlooked. To bring attention to this population, ReUp amplifies the adult learner experience and debunks myths about their abilities, motivations, and barriers to reenrollment and persistence. For instance, many of these former students do want to return to school but have been overlooked in terms of outreach campaigns. We've also learned that academic performance, i.e., low grades, typically is not a major concern for most returners, but finances are (UPCEA, 2023). Working with the returning adult population has given me plenty of insight into the unique experiences of first-gens who also are nontraditional by age or circumstances.

It is generally understood that while they often share common characteristics, first-generation college students are a heterogenous population. But as Longwell-Grice and Longwell-Grice (2021) note, "For too long higher educational professionals have written, thought about, developed policies for, and practiced as if first-generation students are all one and only one identity" (p. xxii). As a result, these students' needs still are not met despite the proliferation of first-generation offices, national celebrations, and good intentions.

To move beyond thinking of first-generation students as a monolith, Longwell-Grice and Longwell-Grice (2021) argue that scholars and practitioners need to challenge the "false idea that all first-gens think, act, and experience things in the same way" (1). In other words, we must value intersectionality, or the notion that first-generation students have a span of identities outside of their educational background that shape their trajectory, such as race, gender, immigration status, and income, to name only a few

(Center for First-generation Student Success, 2017). Longwell-Grice and Longwell-Grice go on to say "it is imperative that higher education professionals acknowledge the complexities of first-gen status as they develop policies and practices that affect first-generation students" to avoid overgeneralizing the population and watering down the support (10). NASPA reports that nearly one-third of all currently enrolled first-generation college students are age 30 or above; however, not much is known about this growing population (Hamilton, 2023). Many services and offices directed at first-generation students, such as freshmen seminars, residential summer bridge programs, and new to career services, particularly those at four-year institutions, over-index on the traditional first-time full-time population. One can reasonably conclude that students who identify as both first-generation to college and an adult learner benefit from valuable services and resources that also reflect their lived experiences and perspectives.

What does it mean to focus on intersectionality among the first-gen population? In this case, we would unpack how first-generation students who also are adult learners either by age demographic (typically age 25 or older) or circumstance (such as caring for others or working full-time) are navigating the college experience. We must consider what is unique about this subpopulation and determine how we can best tailor resources to suit their needs. Even in the Longwell-Grice & Longwell-Grice monograph about first-generation intersectional identities, which covers transfer students, undocumented students, and various racial/ethnic communities, first-gen adult learners are not called out. The field is ripe for discussion.

Although I completed my undergraduate work by age 24, I had adult-like responsibilities while I was in college. I paid for most of my education myself, and I balanced working a minimum of 20 hours a week on top of other commitments. Similarly, after a stint in the Marine Corps fighting in Operation Desert Storm as a 22-year-old college student, my then boyfriend/now husband returned to school full-time and graduated with his undergraduate degree at age 30 becoming the first in his immediate family to do so. Mom, Rob, and I all identify as first-gen adult learners.

While the term "first-generation student" isn't new to higher education, it refers to a segment of the college population that's become a greater focus on many campuses. Fifty-six percent of all postsecondary students in the US are considered first generation college students—that is, they have parents or caregivers who don't hold bachelor's degrees (Hamilton, 2023). First-generation college students often face common barriers, such as weak sense of belonging to the institution and the hidden curriculum within higher education. These potholes typically are compounded for those who navigate as adult learners given that their personal and professional responsibilities, in addition to time away from school, voluntary or not, often puts these students at a social and sometimes academic disadvantage. Adult learners who are first-generation to college also may be more susceptible to social exclusion because they are older than their classmates or have different life experiences, like full-time work or the military. As a result, these students may be unaware of or reluctant to seek or to use resources, like the writing center or well-being services, that are intended to support them (Tyton Partners 2023). Once again, these disconnects may compound adult learners' sense of belonging and may even contribute to attrition and stopping out of the institution.

Even the first-generation to college definition, although important, can create landmines for the target population to maneuver. For instance, the definition relies upon the status of one's parents (Collins & Jehangir, 2021); however, many adult learners are parents themselves or have elderly parents that they care for. Some adult learners may question how this definition or experience is relevant to them, as they very well may be supporting their own college student or younger siblings. The older one is, one may argue, the less impactful one's parental education may be.

To address the unique needs of adult learners who also are first-generation to college, I offer a few suggestions for IHEs of all types and organizations that support this heterogenous group.

REVISIT THE FIRST-GENERATION DEFINITION

To reach *any* first-generation student, it is important to provide a clear definition of the term and to use affirming language when referring to the population, such as "pioneers" or "trailblazers." These terms are critical to overturning deficit framing about the group, such as they lack or do not know things. Instead, these terms are empowering because they are strengths-based. It must be noted that although "first-generation" has become more popularized, it generally reflects a higher education vernacular, and students of any age may not immediately connect with it or fully understand its significance. Also bear in mind that students may use common parlance like "I'm the only one who went to college," "This is/was all new to me," or "No one in my family understands college" to make meaning of their experiences. These student-driven definitions must be validated by staff and administrators. Adult learners who qualify for resources may not see themselves in definitions that stress *their parents'* level of education without some guidance. For instance, adult learners may be in school simultaneously with their children, or their children may have completed BEFORE them, such as the case with Mom and me. As a result, first-generation adult learners add much needed complexity to standard definitions of first-generation to college.

When attempting to identify first-gens, it is important to ask open-opened questions about their identity rather than those that yield a "yes" or "no" response, such as, "Are you a first-generation student?" Ideally, students should have an opportunity to share their educational backgrounds prompted by an open-ended question, i.e., "What is the highest degree that your parent or caregiver obtained?" [if known]. This allows for students to fill in narrative gaps that will provide the institution or organization relevant background information about the student's history, such as degrees or certificates earned outside of the country and non-completed degrees.

Finally, it is necessary to regularly share the first-gen definition throughout the institution or organization, not just during admissions season but throughout an academic year and over the summer. The term could be explained on websites, in handbooks, on relevant applications, and on printed materials, like flyers and brochures. First-generation college awareness exists on a spectrum, and it may take a student, particularly an adult student who may be unaccustomed to being identified as a dependent, some time to connect with the identity for some of the reasons mentioned previously.

BUILD COMMUNITIES AND GET OUT OF THE WAY

Given their age and prior experience, it may be presumed that adult learners do not seek support and therefore are at risk of being overlooked and left to navigate independently. Connect adult learners to first-gen services, including those that are place based and those that are online. In 2016, I voluntarily established a Facebook group, Empowering First Generation Students, following a presentation at the annual First Year Experience (FYE) conference in Dallas, Texas. At the time, it was rare to find sessions specifically on the first-generation college population. Intended for the 25 conference participants only, the group has grown to over 7,500 community members and has functioned like a de facto virtual resource center. Many of the students in the group are also full-time employees, parents of adult children, caregivers, military veterans, and college returners after long absences, i.e., adult learners. It is common for people to ask questions in the chat that they are nervous to ask their own campus academic advisors, financial aid counselors, and college instructors. On the first day of class, Alexis A. began to worry about the workload in a particular course and turned to the Facebook group for options:

> The reason I'm considering [dropping a class] is because the professor has a crazy workload and has super high expectations. I am in community college full time but still do have a job. My concern is that I won't be able to keep up and would rather drop it now then fail later. How would I go about dropping a class? Would I be able to take the same course with a different professor? Can this affect my [FAFSA] eligibility?

Within hours, a variety of people, including tenured faculty, academic advisors, and current students chimed in with advice and affirmations. Other group members have shared milestones that they feel won't be well-received amongst family. For instance, Elizabeth, a mother of three, shared her excitement in the group: "Guys I just found out that I got a scholarship for next semester! Wanted so badly to tell my parents, but they don't care. Just wanted to share my good news with someone. . . It feels absolutely amazing to be celebrated for once."

Student-oriented Facebook groups like these point to an unexpected resource: social media and digital communities (Felton et al., 2023; Rowan-Kenyon et al., 2018). If first-generation centers are not specifically targeting the adult learner population and their needs, it makes sense that those students would turn to an accessible alternative like a Facebook group where people typically respond within minutes. Digital communities like Facebook groups, Discord channels, and even Instagram accounts can be powerful resources, especially for adult learners who must fit school into their busy lives. These are good places to share resources like upcoming events and application deadlines and to build community via discussions and chats. With some encouragement, students may take ownership of the spaces and speak in their own voices directly to their peers. Finally, whether online or in person, whenever possible, include family (broadly defined) and chosen family that might close friends or co-workers.

ATTACK THE HIDDEN CURRICULUM

A common challenge that all types of first-generation students often face is navigating the hidden curriculum of higher education, i.e., the rules and behaviors that students are expected to know but are not taught or shown directly (Gable, 2022; Margolis, 2001). For instance, academia is known for its jargon. Obscure words like "bursar," "matriculation," "prerequisite," and "registrar" often confound students, as well as acronyms and other college lingo. Those individuals who haven't been through the college experience or who may have gaps in their education journey may find it challenging to understand this terminology, and therefore leave questions unanswered. Adult learners may feel uninformed, given their time away from school. Offering an on-site website translation service is one way to address this barrier; for example, Georgia Tech's Office of Student Integrity implemented Google and Bing translator into its site. Other schools, such as Middle Georgia State University and Delaware County Community College have created online "jargon glossaries" to help level the playing field.

With an increased understanding of the motivations and struggles of adult learners who are first-generation college students, institutions of higher learning have a real opportunity to adjust their policies, programs, and resources so that this population is on track for personal and professional success.

NOTES

1. Parts of this essay are derived by a blog post that I wrote for the ReUp Education website.
2. The federal government defines "first-generation college" as neither parent or guardian has obtained a four-year degree (Higher Education Act, 1965).
3. The National Clearinghouse reports that 2.1% of stopped out students re-enroll (p. 7).

REFERENCES

Bahr, P. R. (2012). Student flow between community colleges: Investigating lateral transfer. *Research in Higher Education, 53*(1), 94–121. https://doi-org.libproxy.scu.edu/10.1007/s11162-011-9

Center for First-generation Student Success. (2017, December 1). *First-generation students: Approaching enrollment, intersectional identities, & asset-based success.* https://firstgen.naspa.org/blog/first-generation-students-approaching-enrollment-intersectional-identities-and-asset-based-success

Collins, K. & Jehangir, R. (2021). "It's hard for everybody": Navigating the tensions and tolerance of graduate school as a first-generation scholar. *The Good Society: A Journal of Civic Studies, 30*(1–2), 48–70.

Felton, P., Lambert, L. M., Artze-Vega, I. & Miranda Tapia, O. R. (2023). *Connections are everything: A college student's guide to relationship-rich education.* Johns Hopkins University Press.

Gable, R. (2022). *The hidden curriculum: First generation students at legacy universities.* Princeton University Press.

Higher Education Act. (1965). Federal TRIO programs. In L.- Grice, (Ed.), *At the intersection: Understanding and supporting first-generation students* (pp. 301–312). Stylus Publishing.

Hamilton, I. (2023, June 13). 56% of all undergraduates are first-generation college students. *Forbes.* https://www.forbes.com/advisor/education/online-colleges/first-generation-college-students-by-state/

Katsinas, S., Bray, N., Hagedorn, L., Dotherow, S., & Malley, M. (2019). From vertical to dynamic transfer: Recognizing continuous Swirl in American higher education. *Change, 51*(3), 44–51. https://doi.org/10.1080/00091383.2019.1606607

Klein-Collins, R., & Framularo, C. (2022, January). *Attracting adult learners with credit for prior learning. A CAEL/Strada Research brief.* Council for Adult and Experiential Learning Report.

Longwell-Grice, R., & Longwell-Grice, H. (Eds.). (2021). *At the intersection: Understanding and supporting first-generation students*. (1st ed.). Routledge.

Margolis, E. (Ed.) (2001), *The hidden curriculum in higher education*. Routledge.

National Student Clearinghouse Research Center. (2023, April). *Some college, No credential student outcomes annual progress report – academic year 2021/22*.

Rodriguez, J. (2024, February 6). *#AdvocateFirstGen through storytelling, center for first- generation student success*. https://firstgen.naspa.org/advocate-firstgen/advocatefirstgen-through-storytelling

Rowan-Kenyon, H., Martinez Aleman, A. M., & Savitz-Romeer, M. (2018). *Technology and engagement: Making technology work for first-generation college students*. Rutgers University Press.

Schmalz, J. (2015, March 25). *How an elite women's college lost its base and found its mission, chronicle of higher education*.

UPCEA. (2023, October). *Disengaged learners & return paths to higher education*. UPCEA.

ADDITIONAL READING

Rease Miles, L. (n.d.). *First-generation, Second chance: Supporting adult learners. ReUp education*. https://reupeducation.com/resources/first-generation-second-chance-supporting-stopout-students-through-a-personal-and-family-milestone/

Shaw, C., Bharadwaj, R., Bryant, G., Condon, K. & Rich, J. (2023). *Driving toward a degree: Awareness, belonging, and coordination*. Tyton Partners.

CHAPTER 5

UNLOCKING AUTHENTIC D.E.I.B. LEADERSHIP IN ADULT EDUCATION: LEVERAGING 3 KEYS OF EMOTIONAL INTELLIGENCE IN THE WORKPLACE

Airies Davis
Dominican University and etiKID Academy LLC, USA

ABSTRACT

Can you be your true self at work, just as you are on the weekend? For many, especially those from marginalized communities, this is a complex challenge. This chapter defines authentic leadership as "the unobstructed operation of one's true- or core-self in one's daily enterprise" (Kernis & Goldman, 2006, p. 294) and expands on this by describing it as unfiltered actions and behaviors without fear of consequences. The chapter explores the intersection of authenticity and emotional intelligence (EI or EQ) within the context of diversity, equity, inclusion, and belonging (D.E.I.B.) in the workplace. Emotional intelligence—the ability to understand and manage emotions—is a vital component of authentic leadership (Goleman, 2020). As identified by the World Economic Forum (2020), EI is among the top ten skills for the future workforce. Through a descriptive narrative rooted in lived experience as a Black woman in the workplace, this chapter offers practical strategies for adult learners to unlock authentic D.E.I.B. leadership. Using Daniel Goleman's EI framework, it highlights three key elements—self-awareness, relationship management, and social awareness—that promote inclusive leadership. This chapter encourages a deeper understanding of how emotional intelligence enables more authentic and equitable leadership within adult education and professional environments.

Keywords: Emotional intelligence; social awareness; relationship management; self-awareness, and authentic leadership

INTRODUCTION

Despite the forthcoming notable accolades and transformative experiences gained throughout my academic and career pathways, consider the burden of feeling compelled to wear a metaphorical mask every day, concealing aspects of edit to one's true self, even without the presence of a political, racial, and global pandemic and economic crisis (Avolio, B. et al., 2024). This is my reality and the reality for many individuals, particularly those from diverse cultural backgrounds, who navigate the complexities of adult education and workplace dynamics while grappling with the pressure to conform to dominant norms and expectations. The metaphorical mask serves as a protective shield, shielding vulnerable aspects of identity from potential scrutiny, discrimination, or misunderstanding. It represents the effort to assimilate, adapt, or conform to prevailing cultural norms and expectations, often at the expense of authenticity and belonging or relatedness needs without the feeling of ostracism (Haldorai et al., 2020). In this chapter, I invite you to reflect on the environments, whether within organizational or academic settings, where expressing your authentic self is genuinely encouraged. This request may give many leaders pause and cause some apprehension as you delve inward to examine your leadership dimensions and the factors that have shaped your career journey. I leaned into Daniel Goleman's emotional intelligence theoretical framework, which empower individuals to effectively manage both their own emotions and those of others (Goleman, 2020), as my North-Star or guiding principle when expressing my authentic self as a leader. As we create space for you to explore dimensions of leadership—purpose, values, heart, relationships, and self-discipline—like my lived experiences, it is crucial to emphasize your journey and the inspirational figures who have guided our development as authentic leaders (George, 2003). Take a moment to take stock of your physical, mental, and emotional state of being in context of authentic leadership in adult education.

In this chapter, we will explore how emotional intelligence, specifically the pillars of self-awareness, relationship management, and social awareness, can serve as powerful tools for unlocking authentic diversity, equity, inclusion, and belonging (DEIB) leadership within the context of adult education in the workplace. Through a deeper understanding of emotional intelligence and its application in leadership, individuals and organizations can create environments where diversity is celebrated, and all voices are heard and respected. Research has consistently shown that leaders with high levels of emotional intelligence are better equipped to cultivate positive relationships, navigate conflicts, and drive meaningful change within their organizations (Goleman, 2020). Moreover, in the context of organizational DEI initiatives, emotional intelligence plays a crucial role in fostering a culture of authenticity, belonging, and respect, where adult learners from diverse backgrounds feel valued and empowered to contribute their unique perspectives (Goleman, 2020). The academic and career pathways outlined below will illustrate my journey and lessons as an adult learner toward authentic leadership in the workplace utilizing the emotional intelligence tenants of self-awareness and relationship management as the driver.

PATHWAYS

The forthcoming journey exploration aims to illuminate the academic and career pathways that have shaped my lived experiences and established me as a Black woman Diversity, Equity/Equality, Inclusion, and Belonging (D.E.I.B.) thought-leader, navigating in executive level roles predominately held by white male and female leaders. Through this narrative, I will offer insights into the rigor and challenges I have overcome to reach a place of confidence and comfort in exhibiting my authentic leadership and high emotional intelligence in the workplace. Additionally, I will delve into the strategies and approaches I have employed as an adult learner and leader to navigate and thrive within environments where my identity and perspective may diverge from the Eurocentric norm, ultimately contributing to a more inclusive and diverse organizational culture.

Academic Pathway

I was born in the rural South before relocating to Chicago, Illinois, to complete my elementary through high school academic journey. I grew up in a low socio-economic housing project called LeClaire Courts, on the Southwest side of Chicago. This demographic notation is significant to my academic and career trajectory of persistence and leadership fortitude.

Throughout my adolescent years, I was raised by a loving and hardworking two parent household. Both my mom and stepdad often worked two jobs to financially support me and my younger sister. I gained independence and leadership skills early on as a latch-key kid, symbolized by the key I wore around my neck, indicating my role and responsibility for safety, dinner, and homework after school. Despite growing up amidst traumas in my neighborhood, I saw beauty in the small things. Befittingly, my mother ensured that our home was not just safe but also aesthetically pleasing, winning accolades for our impeccably cared-for lawn. Her dedication to maintaining beauty mirrored my own resilience in finding positivity and persistence in challenging environments.

Despite the socioeconomic barriers, I was an academically high achiever, testing successfully into a selective enrollment Chicago Public School, Lindblom Math and Science Academy, a college preparatory high school. I faced a myriad of barriers including access to human capital and educational resources (Davidson et al., 2020). I grasped the significance of earning top grades yet struggled to overcome the racial biases ingrained in standardized testing. My mother, who earned her General Educational Development and later an Associate's degree, instilled in me the belief that education served as the great equalizer. Education was an achievement no one could take away once completed. Thus, it became imperative for me not only to excel academically but also to serve as a role model for my siblings and cousins. Despite dedicating extensive effort, time, and focus to studying for standardized tests, I found myself unable to connect with questions that failed to reflect my cultural background. This left me feeling disheartened and defeated. However, a pivotal moment of guidance and access emerged, the TRIOS Summer Bridge program at the University of Illinois Urbana Champaign (UIUC) offered a supportive community of peers and invaluable resources that bolstered my resilience and propelled me toward achieving my undergraduate academic aspirations. These lived experiences as an emerging leader were instrumental in bolstering my self-efficacy as an adult learner, revealing that one's journey can be enriched and transformed through equitable access. This understanding has been instrumental in guiding my career decisions as an adult learner (Arghode et al., 2021).

Furthermore, I gained confidence and fortitude to persist, and now I am a proud first generation graduate, on my matriarch's side of the family, to earn a doctorate degree. To complement my professional experiences, I earned a doctorate in educational psychology and a master's in business administration (MBA). Immediately after completing my MBA, I moved to Los Angeles to attend the University of Southern California (USC), sign unseen and without ever stepping foot on campus prior to my graduate student enrollment.

Social factors such as family, peer mentoring, teachers, and friends played a crucial role in shaping many positive outcomes in my life. I successfully integrated learned behavioral changes, such as engaging in peer mentorship, participating in study groups, and seeking support when needed, which have significantly impacted my life's direction (Bandura & Hall, 2018).

I even cofounded the JENGA Doctoral Association with eight Black women, alongside holding leadership positions such as president in several student organizations, including the Rossier Student Organization (RSO) and the Education Doctoral Student Association (EDSA). These academic accomplishments and experiences have deeply influenced my outlook on leadership, highlighting the importance of resilience, determination, and a steadfast commitment to surmounting challenges.

Career Pathway

My career pathway in workforce development spans over 15 years, encompassing roles in both academia and the corporate sector. In corporate, I served as the Assistant Vice President of Corporate Recruiting and Senior Client Adoption Trainer for Fortune 500 organizations. Yet, my career journey in higher education is not traditional. I started part-time as an Adjunct Instructor teaching a career development pathways course and an Executive in Residence, in the business school, providing workforce resources to current students and alumni. While nontraditional, my year of experiential learning transcends across both corporate and academic sectors. Thus, a Hispanic Serving Institution of Higher Education. I am charged with strategically developing and maintaining multiyear credit and noncredit courses-certificates, workforce training programs, and lifelong learning catalogs aligned with the collective mission social and structural determinants for marginalized communities, with an emphasis on Black and Brown adult student populations. In alignment with Meyerson's (2003) concept of tempered radicals, described as individuals who skillfully navigate between conformity and rebellion, I embraced the role because I sought to uphold my own values and identity system, even in the face of incongruence with prevailing academic cultures (Buchanan, 2020).

Additionally, I am recognized as an award-winning thought leader for my expertise in emotional intelligence, career planning, and workforce development. Throughout my career, I have led and designed 8-hour full-day research-based adult learning workshops for a diverse range of clients, including educational institutions, corporations, and government entities. These workshops have covered a wide array of topics, including but not limited to workforce development, social justice, emotionally intelligent leadership, diverse supplier partnerships, gender equity, racism, power and privilege, and the intricacies of diversity mapping and scorecards.

One notable project involved collaborating with to support a Big four consulting firm, City Colleges, and a Package Carrier in designing and implementing a scalable career pathway model. This project yielded several significant outcomes, including alignment of employers' skill demands with local postsecondary, vocational, and Career and Technical Education training and certification offerings. Additionally, it fostered partnerships between employers and training partners for associates at employers' worksites, as well as partnerships with City Colleges to create and implement a monitoring and evaluation framework tracking return on investments (ROI) and key performance indicators (KPIs) for adult learners. These initiatives aim to bridge the educational gap between workforce demands and available training opportunities, fostering a more seamless transition for individuals seeking to enter or advance within the workforce.

The project also led to the creation and execution of a scalable model for entering the marketplace. Various student groups, especially Black women, confront distinct and frequently more significant obstacles during their higher education pursuits compared to other demographics (Bush et al., 2023). Recognizing these dynamics has profoundly shaped my experiences and informs my efforts in promoting adult education. I am deliberate in my approach to supporting all populations, with an emphasis on diverse groups, in my professional endeavors. I ensure all are appropriately acknowledged and seen for their respective contributions. I even make it a priority to ensure that every voice is not only heard but also duly recognized, thereby avoiding the misattribution barriers of bias. This includes situations where credit for ideas generated by women or culturally diverse groups is incorrectly assigned or taken by others, as well as avoiding essentializing or categorizing stereotypical traits or qualities to marginalized populations. I have personally witnessed and bravely called out these occurrences real time.

EXPERIENCES

DEI Research-Self & Social Awareness

In the workplace, the pressure to wear a metaphorical mask daily, concealing aspects of your true self can be especially pronounced, as individuals strive to navigate professional environments where cultural differences may not always be understood or valued. For many diverse cultures, especially Black people, the decision to remove the mask and reveal one's authentic self is reserved for moments of trust and intimacy, where we feel safe and accepted. For many of us, in the workplace, fostering spaces with social awareness that allows individuals to bring their authentic selves and cultivate intimacy can lead to increased satisfaction and productivity. Diverse cultures employ various behaviors to cultivate trust, develop possible selves, and foster a professional image in the workplace (McCluney et al., 2021). However, the pervasive need to maintain this facade can contribute to feelings of alienation, imposter syndrome, and disconnection from colleagues and organizational culture. My journey in adult education began with esteemed Fortune 500 firms such as Merrill Lynch and Deloitte. These spaces did not embrace bringing one's authentic self, including natural hair and culturally representative attire, to the workplace. Despite challenges, I remained steadfast. I proudly wore my natural hair coils, often encountering resistance from white leaders who deemed it unprofessional. Picture your manager justifying disciplinary action against you and asking you to change your natural hair and braided styles, simply for you being authentically yourself in the workplace and subtly suggesting that you conform to white societal norms. Being authentic in the workplace required strategic navigation. Bravely, I stood firm in my refusal to conform. It is important to note that the CROWN Act or (Creating a Respectful and Open World for Natural Hair), legislation aimed to address and prohibit hair discrimination based on race and ethnicity, particularly against Black individuals and people of color, was not yet a reality at that time. These experiences underscores the importance of fostering inclusive workplaces where individuals feel empowered to bring their whole selves to work, free from fear of judgment or reprisal.

By acknowledging and addressing the challenges associated with wearing this metaphorical mask, individuals, and organizations, especially in adult education, can cultivate environments where diversity is celebrated, and authentic expression is embraced. But how? Let us explore three methods to unlock authentic DEI leadership utilizing emotional intelligence: *self-awareness, relationship management,* and *social awareness,* and how they relate to leadership, fostering a more equitable and diverse workplace (Goleman, 2020). The chapter aims to create a safe space to foster a deeper understanding of one's own emotions, strengths, and areas for growth, by amplifying my personal experiences, allowing you to reference my lived experience to help you lead more authentically in the context of adult education in the workplace.

Leadership Experiences-Relationship Management

One transformative leadership experience that significantly influenced my personal growth, and the relationship management tenant of emotional intelligence development, was cofounding the JENGA Doctoral Association (JENGA or JDA) at USC alongside eight Black women. Our primary objective was to achieve a one hundred percent degree completion rate for students pursuing doctoral degrees. This experience underscored the vital role of peer mentorship, community support, and innovative strategies in adult education. These experiences highlighted the importance of fostering inclusive and supportive environments for academic success and personal growth. Research indicates that degree attainment for Black women increases by approximately twenty percent annually compared to White and Asian women (Bush et al., 2023). Recognizing the statistical disparities in doctoral degree completion and the lack of clear career pathways post-graduation, JENGA was initially established as a mastermind group focused on providing a safe university recognized student support group for persistence and business development. As our journey continued, it became increasingly clear that there was a pressing need to prioritize our social and emotional well-being and establish a safe space for authentic relationships as adult learners. Many of us encountered challenges related to balancing, rejuvenating or, in some cases, restarting our careers amid evolving life changes such as shifting family dynamics, financial constraints, adapting to new learning styles, births, deaths, and relocating to new cities. Despite these challenges as adult learners, we bonded and even cried at times under the common thread of recognizing our strengths such as shared life experience, motivation, and clear career goals. These shared experiences contributed to our collective successful academic and personal growth outcomes. By leveraging peer mentorship, we held each other accountable, with tough love and no excuses to accomplish our coursework and dissertation goals (Butler, 2023). Being an adult learner can be isolating. The authentic sisterhood and support system provided by JENGA proved invaluable throughout the journey, ensuring that all eight women achieved a one hundred percent degree completion rate and mitigating many of the academic, social, financial, and career challenges we faced along the way.

Another transformative leadership experience unfolded during my tenure as the Chicago chapter president of the National Association of African Americans in Human Resources (NAAAHR). NAAAHR serves as a platform for mentorship, education, and career guidance, offering a unique global forum for the professional development of Black and African American adult human resources learners. Through a serendipitous encounter with a mentor-turned-friend at a wedding, I gained invaluable insight into the significance of participating in board leadership within professional associations and its pivotal role in driving systematic and cultural transformation toward inclusivity and belonging in both corporate and academic settings (Cummings, 2022). Little did I know, this mentor held an executive position at one of the leading Big

4 professional services consulting firms. Emphasizing the importance of lifelong learning, my mentor encouraged me to embrace new challenges at any stage of life. The mentor shared his journey as a Black man, emphasizing the biases, emotional regulation requirements, and challenges of being the first or only person of color to achieve C-suite and partner level success in numerous corporate environments. As an adult learner stepping into organizational and professional association board leadership later in life, I initially grappled with imposter syndrome as a first-time executive board leader, influenced in part by exposure to leading influencers in the HR space (Fields & Cunningham-Williams, 2021). Guided by mentors and drawing from self confidence and authentic lived experiences as a Black woman, I swiftly embraced and acknowledged my innate people skills. These experiences marked my initial foray into understanding the importance of embracing leadership and taking on responsibilities, especially when others recognize and celebrate it in you.

While the list of significant leadership experiences is not exhaustive, a pivotal moment occurred when I assumed my senior executive role at Merrill Lynch. Another crucial lesson learned as an adult learner was the importance of effectively managing not only my emotions but also those of others, using the relationship management tenant in emotional intelligence to navigate complex career decisions and leadership dynamics. As the Assistant Vice President of Corporate Recruiting for the capital markets division, I found myself entrusted with significant responsibilities, including overseeing direct reports and dotted line responsibilities for various business lines, all under the purview of reporting directly to the Chief Financial Officer. However, achieving the right title, fair compensation, and even an office proved to be a challenging endeavor as a Black woman, despite the confidential nature of my role and the critical nature of my interactions. As adult learners with years of professional experience, assumptions are frequently made about our level of expertise and abilities in performing the job. It is often suggested that we are either overqualified or lacking updated and relevant technical skills. As an young and emerging leader, I fell victim to believing those assumptions were accurate despite my reality. Although I was initially thrilled to be considered for the position, I failed to recognize my own value and the importance of showing up authentically. It is worth noting that despite my extensive experience and tenure with Big 4 consulting firms and a top-tier education, senior leadership initially attempted to assign me a lesser title without justification. Being influenced by my inner saboteur, or the inner voice that diminishes self-worth, I was even on the verge of accepting the lower title and compensation package. Fortunately, my sponsors and advisors, played a crucial role in coaching and advocating for my voice, one particularly was another

Black woman in a senior leadership role. Without their support, advocacy, sponsorship, and understanding the significance relationship management, I might have continued to feel voiceless. My experience serves as a compelling example of the importance of relationship management, an essential tenet of emotional intelligence, which emphasizes the ability to coach, mentor, and effectively navigate conflicts (Jackson, 2023). In today's dynamic and diverse workplace landscape, the importance of emotional intelligence (EI) in fostering inclusive environments and effective leadership for adult learners cannot be overstated. Not only did I achieve the executive title, compensation, and corner office, but I also earned the respect of my manager, the Chief Financial Officer, who extended an invitation to join leadership meetings, including with the Chief Executive Office, typically reserved for more tenured leaders.

REFLECTION

This section will offer a reflective analysis of the advice I would impart to myself as a burgeoning leader in higher education and corporate, both in the past and present. Throughout this narrative, I will delve into pivotal moments of growth and highlight milestone achievements, drawing from my journey in academia and the corporate sector to provide a comprehensive perspective on my leadership development and lived experiences as a Black woman. Additionally, I will explore how my experiences in both realms have contributed to shaping my leadership style and approach, offering valuable insights for aspiring leaders in the field.

Reflection: Then

Reflecting on the advice I would give myself as an adult learner and Black woman leader in both the higher education and corporate sectors, one significant area where I would urge myself to make a change is to pursue internal leadership positions earlier in my career journey. Despite initially transitioning into academia from a nontraditional corporate or business sector background and harboring doubts about the transferability of my qualifications, I now recognize the value of trusting in my abilities and seizing leadership opportunities. For example, while on the career track toward the C-suite, I resigned from a blue-chip Fortune 500 organization and moved across the country to an unfamiliar campus to pursue my doctorate in education. As an adult learner with family, personal life, and financial responsibilities, this was a significant risk, but essential to my life goals. I recognized by embracing my unique background and perspectives as an adult learner,

I can bring fresh insights and innovative approaches to leadership roles within the academic setting.

Furthermore, I would counsel myself to actively seek out mentorship and support from colleagues and peers who can offer guidance and encouragement as I navigate my leadership journey as an adult learner (Butler, 2023). Correspondingly, I would prioritize continuous learning and professional development, seeking opportunities to expand my skills and knowledge in areas relevant to higher education leadership. By embracing my capabilities and stepping confidently into leadership positions, I can make a meaningful impact within the field of higher education and contribute to positive change within my institution and beyond. Equally, I would advise adult learners to leverage their years of wisdom and diverse cultural experiences. Begin by creating your career playbook, which should assess what is important to you professionally and personally, in order to create a roadmap to achieve your professional and personal goals. Outline and anticipate any potential gaps, barriers, and opportunities, considering the resources needed, and start seeking support before embarking on your journey. Then, have a candid conversation with yourself about your emotional regulation and mindset. Ask yourself: what do I need to remove any emotional triggers, or negative outputs, before they become impactful? How can I embrace glimmers, or small moments of positivity, as inspiration? Finally, remember that your journey is unique, so lean into the plethora of experiences you have gained as an adult learner. Embracing both challenges and successes is an integral part of the process of unlocking your authenticity.

Reflection: Now

Embarking on a journey in higher education leadership, especially as a Black woman, can be both exhilarating and daunting, filled with opportunities for growth and moments of reflection. As I reflect on my own experiences and the lessons learned along the way, I am compelled to share valuable insights and considerations that have shaped my path and influenced my perspective on career development. Embracing one's identity unapologetic for me as a Black women in this realm of leadership is paramount. Equally, acknowledging the unique perspectives, experiences, and contributions can lead to enrichment in the your field and drive positive change. Seeking peer mentorship, sponsorship, and support from other Black women leaders and allies can offer invaluable guidance, encouragement, and perspective, fostering a sense of belonging and empowerment. Advocating for oneself and actively pursuing opportunities for growth and advancement within the field is essential, recognizing that one's goals, aspirations, and needs are worthy of pursuit. Navigating challenges with resilience, perseverance, and a growth mindset, or the belief in your intellect and abilities through dedicated hardwork, is key. This viewpoint allows one to view obstacles as opportunites for learning, growth, and personal development. Finally, prioritizing self-care and well-being is fundamental to sustaining a fulfilling career journey, emphasizing the importance of maintaining a health work-life balance and habits, while nurturing practices that replenish the mind, body, and soul. As I reflect on my journey and the wisdom gained along the way as a Black woman, I am inspired to share pieces of advice from my past and present self within adult education and navigating the workplace landscape leveraging emotional intelligence.

In summary, reflecting on my career journey, both then and now, I have identified several pieces of advice for adult learners. One significant recommendation involves being intentional about shifting focus toward emotional intelligence practices, managing your emotions and those of others by embedding social awareness, relationship management, and self-awareness tenants. I believe this can serve as a guided strategy to unlock authenticity and embark on a diverse leadership journey in the workplace (Gonzales, 2022). These reflective practices would be invaluable for adult learners to gain an understanding of their past and present selves. Correspondingly, this insight might lead to different actions in the following reflective outcomes:

> Embrace my identity: I would advise myself to embrace my identity as a Black woman in higher education leadership from the outset. My proclamation when faced with imposter syndrome, or self-doubt, is recite "I am an unapologetic and unashamed Black women" on a mission to transform the workplace with emotionally intelligent adult learners. This statement allows me to recognize that my unique perspective, experiences, and contributions are valuable assets that can enrich the field and drive positive change. In adult education, your wisdom and insight are valued, mainly because of the expertise and tenure you bring. Refrain from shying away, instead embrace your unique identity and perspective.
>
> Seek out mentorship and support: I would encourage myself to actively seek out mentorship and support from other Black women leaders and allies in higher education. You may question how do I gain support when access to the sea of Black women leaders in higher education is shallow and limiting. Exercise intentionality in how you engage in relationship centered encounters is key. As adult learners, it can be intimidating, in some instances, to start over when building connections. Join become active in leadership roles within professional associations and employee resource groups related to your areas of interest and learning. I surrounded myself

with a supportive network of mentors, colleagues, and peers who understood and shared similar and dissimilar experiences which provided invaluable guidance, encouragement, and perspective.

Advocate for myself: I would remind myself to advocate for my own career development and advancement within the field of adult education. I would not hesitate to articulate my goals, aspirations, and needs, and actively seek out opportunities for growth, advancement, and recognition. I recall when I first began my adult education career being overlooked and asked to share my success of revamping career curriculum with a white colleague who did not contribute to the task. I simply refused. This advocacy stance led to the department chairs reviewing discrepancies in how all leaders, including Black women, were rewarded and revising the process for collaborative work.

Navigate challenges with resilience: I recognize that as a Black woman in higher education leadership, we may encounter unique challenges and obstacles along the way. I recommend approaching these challenges bravely with resilience, perseverance, persistence, and an emotionally intelligent growth mindset, viewing them as opportunities for learning, growth, and personal development.
In adult education, the status quo often becomes normalized, especially for Black women. Many prefer to maintain the historical legacy of the higher education institution, believing that traditional fixed methods, which oftentimes tend to advantage White populations, are the only viable approach to getting the job done. While history is important, determine what career legacy or footprint you want to leave in your educational institution. And, consider how your unique perspective and lived experiences, can open the doors for difficult workplace conversations in adult education.

Prioritize self-care: Lastly, I would prioritize self-care and well-being as essential components of my career development journey. I recognize the importance of embedding daily healthy work-life balance, including setting boundaries, and prioritizing self-care practices that nourish and replenish my physical, emotional, and mental well-being. My often-used slogan when setting boundaries states "no is a complete sentence." In adult education, as Black women, we are often stretched to work in areas in and outside of our departments without equitable compensation. Recently my educational institution created a day of self-care where adult learners were encouraged in a collective workplace community setting to create art, exercise, eat health foods, and meditate. This experience affirmed the institutions commitment to self-care. Yet, it was up to the adult learners to unplug to take advantage of the resources offered.

ADVICE

Self-Awareness

In adult education, the first tip is to cultivate self-awareness as an essential emotional intelligence tool for navigating the complexities of leadership roles effectively. Developing self-awareness begins with a commitment to introspection and reflection (Goleman, 2020). I would encourage leaders in adult education to take time for self-reflection and gain insight into strengths, weaknesses, and values, which in turn informs their leadership approach. For example, create your leadership story or headline by identifying key skills and traits reflective of who you are now and where you want to go in your future workplace journey. My headline states in part "I am a multihyphenated strategist with advance leadership skills in workforce development and organizational transformation". Equally, I take stock of where I am in my leadership journey by conducting a listening tour and asking informed questions from my peers. This ability to seek feedback advice from peers, mentors, and team members provides leaders in adult education with valuable perspectives on how their behavior and decisions impact others.

Moreover, I would highly encourage practicing mindfulness through meditation or journaling to further deepen self-awareness and enhance emotional regulation, enabling leaders in adult education to navigate challenges with clarity and composure. These mindfulness practices can be as incremental as 30 sec to five-minute pauses throughout the day where you practice breathing exercises, cite affirmations, or simply unplug to notice and appreciate your surroundings. By prioritizing self-awareness, adult learners can harness their unique insights and experiences to drive positive change and foster inclusive environments where all individuals can thrive. The following are tips to employ to gain a heightened level of self-awareness:

Take time for self-reflection: Encourage leaders to regularly reflect on their thoughts, feelings, and actions to gain insight into their strengths, weaknesses, and values in adult education. In adult education, you are often juggling multiple tasks in the workplace. This pause creates space for self-care and introspection.

Seek feedback: Encourage leaders to actively seek feedback from peers, mentors, and team members to gain an understanding of how their behavior and decisions impact others in adult education. This includes identifying a sample size of trusted advisors and asking them to share in three minutes what attributes do they most admire in your leadership skills. It is important to actively listen,

without intent to respond, in order to gain the most value from this exercise.
- Practice mindfulness: Encourage leaders to engage in mindfulness practices such as meditation or journaling to cultivate self-awareness and emotional regulation in adult education. One personal favorite is my mindful three-minute exercise where first you take one minute to take a deep breath in for 10 seconds, hold for 10 seconds and breathe out for 10 seconds. Then immediately move to writing, listening, or reading based a on a positive resource for learning. Finally, the remaining minute is used to sit silently in reflection observing your immediate surroundings for items that bring you joy and peace.

Relationship Management

Navigating relationships in the workplace can be particularly nuanced for culturally diverse and Black women leaders, we often face unique challenges and dynamics in adult education. Adult education is often considered a second chance to gain exposure to workforce development and skill building opportunities. Essentially, adult learners may be building new relationships in classroom and workplace. This can be seen as challenging to start over, especially with budding new and oftentimes unfamiliar relationships. I recall a similar experience when transitioning as an adult learner into my executive MBA program. I did not have prior relationships or experiences with my classmates prior to enrollment, which felt intimidating. Thus, enhancing relationship management skills is another emotional intelligence essential for fostering inclusive and supportive environments in adult education. For example, when considering when and how to foster relationship management, I focus on authentic connections. As a Black women leader, I must prioritize building trust and rapport with team members by demonstrating approachability, transparency, and empathy in my communication and interactions (Cummings, 2022). Creating a culture of open communication is equally important, as it allows adult learners to feel valued and heard, enabling them to express their ideas, concerns, and feedback without fear of judgment or reprisal.

Equally important to relationship management in adult education is providing training and support to help leaders develop effective conflict resolution skills. The mere act of being an adult learner, is nuanced. Many are often faced with difficult conversations and decisions around topics such as work life balance, staying motivated, and problem solving in adult education. Crucial skills in active listening, empathy, and negotiation, support in addressing conflicts, decision making, relationship building, and disagreements constructively (Torres & Davis, 2020). By prioritizing relationship management, we can create workplaces and learning communities where leaders feel empowered, respected, and able to fully contribute our talents and perspectives. The following short list provides methods to enhance relationship management in adult education:

> Build trust and rapport: Encourage leaders to prioritize building trust and rapport with team members by being approachable, transparent, and empathetic in their communication and interactions in adult education. One method is to create grounding norms on how to build rapport with team members. This may include insuring all voices are heard in meetings and creating a safe space to share grievances without negative consequences.
> Foster open communication: Encourage leaders to create a culture of open communication where team members feel comfortable expressing their ideas, concerns, and feedback in adult education. One of the benefits of engaging with adult learners is their breathe of knowledge. Thus, open communication includes adult learners being able to bring unique perspectives to the table with the intent for full consideration and possibly application of the recommendation.
> Resolve conflicts effectively: Provide training and support to help leaders develop conflict resolution skills, such as active listening, empathy, and negotiation, to address conflicts and disagreements constructively in adult education. Hiring managers seek empathic leaders with capacity to solve conflicts and relationship manage in the workplace. Professional development or training to support conflict resolution in adult education is a transferrable skill in the workplace.

Social Awareness

Social awareness is a crucial skill for leaders, especially for Black women who often navigate intersecting identities and social dynamics in the workplace. Cultivating social awareness involves actively listening to others, asking clarifying questions, and demonstrating empathy and understanding for an individuals cultural experiences and life journey. For Black women leaders, this means recognizing and valuing our diverse perspectives, experiences, and voices within their teams and organizations. I recall being asked as the only leader of color to spearhead a diversity initiative while in my MBA program. The faculty who requested this task assumed because of my cultural identity I would be able to solve all of the universities embedded challenges with recruiting and retaining diverse learners. I chose to ask other adult learners, from varied multicultural, racial, and gender background in our cohort to join me in creating a diversity recruitment event requiring the faculty to visible and financially commit to participating in the program. Prioritizing diversity and inclusion efforts is essential, as it fosters environments where all individuals, regardless of background, feel seen, heard, and respected (Torres & Davis, 2020). Essentially, staying informed about social and cultural issues affecting our campus community and society at large allows leaders to consider how these issues impact our leadership decisions and actions, ultimately contributing to more equitable and inclusive workplaces. By cultivating social awareness, leaders can drive positive change, advocate for marginalized communities, and create environments where everyone can thrive. Here are practical strategies to cultivate social awareness as a leader:

- Practice active listening: Encourage leaders to practice active listening by fully engaging with others, asking clarifying questions, and demonstrating empathy and understanding in adult education. Similar to the above example from my MBA program, I recommend to actively ask clarifying questions and do not make assumptions about the skills and interest level, and segment or group individuals of the audience based on their cultural identity.
- Promote diversity and inclusion: Encourage leaders to prioritize diversity and inclusion efforts by actively seeking out diverse perspectives, creating inclusive environments, and addressing bias and discrimination in adult education. It is important to understand the multicultural perspectives adult learners can bring to the workplace. Create a space where their learning is matured and encourage while maintaining awareness of conscious and unconscious bias and discriminatory practices.
- Stay informed about social issues: Encourage leaders to stay informed about social and cultural issues affecting their campus community and society at large, and to consider how these issues impact their leadership decisions and actions in adult education. Curate a repository of resources related to social justice and culturally responsive practices. By providing this type of access to adult learners, there is a creation of support systems.

By prioritizing the tenets of emotional intelligence, including self-awareness, relationship management, and social awareness, new and potential higher education leaders can unlock an authentic leadership in adult education. By cultivating strong relationships, fostering a positive organizational culture, and effectively leading teams to success, these leaders can make significant strides in the field of higher education and beyond. Moreover, embracing these principles can unlock authentic D.E.I.B. leadership in adult education, paving the way for inclusive and equitable learning environments.

CONCLUSION

In conclusion, unlocking authentic diversity, equity, inclusion, and belonging leadership in adult education requires leveraging the three keys of emotional intelligence: self-awareness, relationship management, and social awareness. By focusing on these essential elements, new and potential higher education and corporate leaders can cultivate a heightened level of authentic leadership. Through self-awareness, leaders can gain insight into our own emotions, values, and biases, allowing them to lead with authenticity and integrity. Additionally, by prioritizing relationship management, leaders can build strong connections with our teams, fostering trust, collaboration, and mutual respect. Furthermore, social awareness enables leaders to recognize and empathize with the diverse perspectives and experiences of others, promoting a culture of inclusion and belonging within the organization.

I ask again based on your understanding from my lived experiences, can you be your authentic or true self at work, just as you are on the weekend? I affirm, yes. By embracing these principles of emotional intelligence, new and potential higher education, you can create positive change, foster a supportive and inclusive organizational culture, and lead our teams to success in the dynamic and ever-evolving field of higher education.

REFERENCES

Arghode, V., Heminger, S., & McLean, G. N. (2021). Career self-efficacy and education abroad: Implications for future global workforce. *European Journal of Training and Development, 45*(1), 1–13.

Avolio, B. J., Gardner, W. L., Walumbwa, F. O., Luthans, F., & May, D. R. (2004). Unlocking the mask: A look at the process by which authentic leaders impact follower attitudes and behaviors. *The Leadership Quarterly, 15*(6), 801–823.

Bandura, A., & Hall, P. (2018). Albert Bandura and social learning theory. *Learning Theories for Early Years Practice, 63*.

Buchanan, N. T. (2020). Researching while Black (and female). *Women & Therapy, 43*(1–2), 91–111.

Bush, V. B., Chambers, C. R. & Walpole, M. B. (Eds.) (2023), *From diplomas to doctorates: The success of Black women in higher education and its implications for equal educational opportunities for all.* Taylor & Francis.

Butler, M. (2023). DO NOT CALL ME MISS. *Still Working While Black: The Untold Stories of Student Affairs Practitioners*, 25.

Cummings, A. R. (2022). *Seated at the table*. Xlibris Corporation.

Davidson, J., Clark, T. B., Ijames, A., Cahill, B. F., & Johnson, T. (2020). African American student perceptions of higher education barriers. *Educational Research Quarterly*, *43*(4), 59–69.

Fields, L. N., & Cunningham-Williams, R. M. (2021). Experiences with imposter syndrome and authenticity at research-intensive schools of social work: A case study on Black female faculty. *Advances in Social Work*, *21*(2/3), 354–373.

George, B. (2003). *Authentic leadership: Rediscovering the secrets to creating lasting value*. Jossey-Bass.

Goleman, D. (2020). *Emotional intelligence*. Bloomsbury Publishing.

Gonzales, M. (2022). Practice guide and strategies to increase EI. In *Emotional intelligence for students, parents, teachers and school leaders: A handbook for the whole school community* (pp. 273–294). Springer Singapore.

Haldorai, K., Kim, W. G., Phetvaroon, K., & Li, J. (2020). Left out of the office "tribe": The influence of workplace ostracism on employee work engagement. *International Journal of Contemporary Hospitality Management*, *32*(8), 2717–2735.

Jackson, T. R. (2023). *The emotional intelligence and conflict management relationship in Black women leaders*.thesis

Kernis, M. H. & Goldman, B. M. (2006). A multicomponent conceptualization of authenticity: Theory and research. *Advances in Experimental Social Psychology*, *38*, 283–357. https://doi.org/10.1016/s0065-2601(06)38006-9

McCluney, C. L., Durkee, M. I., Smith II, R. E., Robotham, K. J., & Lee, S. S. L. (2021). To be, or not to be Black: The effects of racial codeswitching on perceived professionalism in the workplace. *Journal of Experimental Social Psychology*, *97*, 104199.

Meyerson, D. E. (2003). *Tempered radicals: How everyday leaders inspire change at work*. Harvard Business School Press.

Torres, A. & Davis, A. (2020). *Mission matters: World's leading entrepreneurs reveal their top tips to success*.

World Economic Forum, J. (2020). *The future of jobs report 2020* Geneva.report

ADDITIONAL READING

Grant, A. M., & Ashford, S. J. (2008). The dynamics of proactivity at work. *Research in Organizational Behavior*, *28*, 3–34.

Hewlin, P. F., Karelaia, N., Kouchaki, M., & Sedikides, C. (2020). Authenticity at work: Its shapes, triggers, and consequences. *Organizational Behavior and Human Decision Processes*, *158*, 80–82.

CHAPTER 6

CREATIVITY AS A DOCKING STATION FOR A FREER FUTURE: CREATIVE DISPATCHES + RADICAL RE-IMAGININGS FROM BLACK DOCTORAL STUDENTS

Gretchen Rudham
Morgan State University, USA

Jacqueline Hayden
Morgan State University, USA

Rosalind Fleming
Morgan State University, USA

ABSTRACT

This chapter explores the radical potential of creativity as a means of intellectual and personal liberation for Black doctoral students. Led by guides Jacque, Rosalind, and Gretchen, alongside students, artists, and educators, the chapter charts a course through counterimaginaries and unapologetically Black creative educational experiences. Central to this dispatch is the argument that creativity breaks traditional academic constraints, allowing researchers to engage in scholarship that reflects their lived experiences and identities. The discussion critiques the historical dominance of white male theorists, questioning their limited perspectives and the exclusion of marginalized voices from established research traditions. Through personal narratives, including encounters with living archives such as Sister Sylvia, the authors illustrate how storytelling and immersive research contribute to knowledge production beyond rigid institutional frameworks. By reimagining doctoral study as a site of creative resistance, the chapter envisions a future where scholarship embraces diverse methodologies, perspectives, and ways of knowing, forging a freer, more inclusive academic landscape. Ultimately, it advocates for scholarship that not only disrupts exclusionary norms but actively expands the boundaries of knowledge in service of equity and empowerment.

Keywords: Creative resistance; black doctoral scholarship; counterimaginaries; storytelling as research; academic liberation

We welcome you to join us on a creative dispatch for radical reimaginings by and for Black doctoral students. This dispatch into creative galaxies will be led by three layers of guides: three main guides (Jacque, Rosalind, and Gretchen), ten doctoral students, and an outer layer of artists and educators. Our reimaginings began in our doctoral courses and research at an Historically Black College and University (HBCU) and continue to radiate into realms beyond the academy. Student vignettes and their accompanying guide questions light the way as we tap into counter imaginaries (Benjamin, 2024) and "unapologetically Black creative educational experiences" (Patton et al., 2022).

JACQUE: BREAKING CHAINS OF TRADITION

Creativity is freedom. Freedom to break the chains of tradition so that I may conduct research and apply knowledge in ways that connect with my spirit, curiosity, interest, and passion. It means being able to show up in spaces as my authentic Black, woman, lesbian self, doing research that makes an impactful difference for me and people like me. Creativity is the freedom to use my voice to synthesize, apply and make new knowledge that goes out into the world for a multitude of purposes including freeing others, elevating others, and providing access and opportunity for others. It means that while I must know how to conduct research, I am not bound to outdated research processes and products. I can choose. That is freedom in itself. That type of freedom spurs creativity.

Research has rarely been presented to me as a creative process. The focus has always been on the cognitive process, and the methods were mostly the same. The theories and theorists that I was exposed to were mostly the same group of white men. This caused a disconnect for me. As a Black, lesbian woman, I did not see myself and experience in theories and work of the theorists that I was required to study. Many of the theorists were theorizing about human behavior or even women. Aren't I a human? Aren't I a woman? Why was my experience not included in the research? When we focus only on this narrow scope and view of white men, we miss current research and other important perspectives that cross race, culture, and gender lines. The narrow scope of research that I was exposed to was dated and did not include modern methods such as digital media, ethnographic studies, or autoethnographic studies. Looked at through the lens of today, the theorists that I was required to study would most likely not have received IRB approval. Let's take Freud and Piaget for example. Freud mostly studied himself, his patients (mostly middle-aged, white women from Vienna), and only one child who he studied in detail. Piaget studied his three grandchildren. These men formed blanket theories on human behavior based on their studies. The studies of both men were limited, biased, and excluded people of color. Piaget's research did not extend beyond his own grandchildren. Both men were theorizing human behavior with a limited scope, yet their theories and research are still used today. What we ask now is not only what and who has been excluded or hidden from previous research, but also why? Which brings me to challenging what has been said and how research has been conducted before and daring to move forward in unique ways.

A creative doctoral dispatch allows me to delve into people and places intimately connected to me. With permission from and respect for the people, places, and things that I research, I immerse myself into communities that I want to learn more about. People are not merely research subjects, they are living, breathing history. Their stories hold answers to questions we have yet to answer and to problems that we are working to solve. My gift is storytelling. Even when I have to dig for information that has been intentionally hidden or erased, I can use the pieces that I unearth to put together a story.

I had the enchanting experience of encountering a walking, talking archive on a research trip during the spring of 2024. I visited the Mother House of the Sisters of the Holy Family. There I met Sister Sylvia. I learned more from Sister Sylvia's stories than I would ever learn simply looking at artifacts. She gave meaning to the artifacts that we found. Her stories, her presence, and her passion gave me new perspective on my research. While I was just as curious and driven about my original research subject, Henriette Delille, I now knew that Sr. Sylvia Thibodeaux was a founding mother in her own right and I was determined to preserve and elevate her story.

My journey at Morgan State University is the first time that this type of creative freedom has been consistently supported and nurtured. I have cocreated a Manifesto to demand proper working conditions for Black teachers. I coproduced a podcast to elevate the voices and experiences of Black, women teachers. I dreamed of what principal development could and should be for Black women principals. My vision was to provide a communal experience centered on the self-care and professional development needs of Black women. Spring semester 2023, I was introduced to counter-narrative research and storytelling. That was the most exciting and validating experience. The counternarrative research began with autobiographical childhood experiences related to schooling. This was emotional because it pushed me to look inside myself for the story and then the real story. I also had to think about the meaning to my child self and my now adult self, two very different perspectives. Things look different and have different meanings, once you are an adult. In this class we also had to interview someone to get a narrative and find the counter narrative. I chose my mother. This became a healing experience for me and gave me a different perspective on her. I understood my mother's decisions about education for her Black daughters much better when hearing her story about her experiences in a newly integrated school, she was one of two Black students in her Kindergarten class. I spent the summer of 2024 immersed in excavating the hidden and diminished stories of founding Black educators. A team of five Black researchers, led by Dr. Rudham traveled to Washington DC, the Carolinas, Baltimore County, Baltimore, City, New York City, Philadelphia, and New Orleans learning about educators who looked like us and had to resist and persist to do the work that they did. Not only are the stories of people who look like me worthy, they are also needed. These stories are our blueprint. For every product that I created or co-created, I had to read articles, and conduct some traditional research; however, I was not limited to those articles and traditional research. I was encouraged to dream, to imagine and to create products that I was passionate about that demonstrated my mastery of course content and more importantly, can be used to positively impact the condition of people.

There are no limits on what I can be curious and passionate about in my research. There is a place for stories to be told. I can do this through storytelling, creating a website, producing a documentary, creating vlogs, incorporating artistic expression or any other product that I choose to produce. The chains have been broken and the top has been lifted off of the box of dictated processes and products. I want that for more Black creatives who are also doctoral students. My hope is that more professors, colleges, and universities welcome and nurture the Black creative in intellectual spaces. It is one thing to welcome us but quite another to encourage us to be free and to nurture our creative freedom. This is the difference between students who come into programs go through but perhaps do not connect or do not finish and students who connect and are able to thrive in their purpose and passion through their creativity.

When I think of Black creatives in academic spaces that do not acknowledge, respect, and encourage their creativity, the poem "A Dream Deferred" by Langston Hughes comes to mind. Do they want our creativity to "dry up like a raisin in the sun, or fester like a sore? Maybe it just sags like a heavy load. Or does it explode?" The explosion is what we want, but not from frustration of holding back passion and purpose. We want an explosion of ideas mixed with the unique ideas that the creative will bring. There is space for creative explosion, and that space must be expanded and protected.

ROSALIND: DREAMING FREELY + EXPANDING ACCESS

For creativity to occur, an environment must be welcoming, with open arms to receive it. Creativity means new ideas, innovation, and dreaming freely. In many issues within society and education, creativity means finding a solution for them or a path forward that has not been done or that is done differently. Creativity is important during assignments, coursework, and research. Doc studies should be about innovation, finding new perspectives, communicating learning differently, being able to take up space in new ways, and also getting research out to people who may not always have access to it.

A creative doctoral dispatch would begin as creating environments for creativity to exist. For example, we must consider, what are the structures that need to be released in order for new ideas and projects to exist in this space? There is a possibility that we would need to deconstruct ways of displaying knowledge, ask ourselves what knowledge needs to be achieved, as well as what are the barriers which can hold back the genius that every student innately brings with them? In fact, not only is the facilitation of knowledge the goal of each professor, but also the ability to cultivate the creativity in each student is also the standard of success as a professor. This is important because many research students have been taught through America's education system, which is one that has mimicked our workforce development. From matching the assembly line during the industrial revolution to aligning with the needs of professionals and influencing, a requirement of knowing subjects deeply, there has not ever been room for creativity which is, arguably, a trait everyone is born with but is stifled throughout the educational system. Therefore, not only is cultivating an environment for creativity important, but being able to bring this stifled gift back to doc students is a must. The skills needed to do this are important and should be a bar to a successful program and instructor. The ability to bring this gift back out of them includes soft skills such as encouragement, motivation, and praise. It also includes instructional skills such as the professor modeling creativity, shifting their assignments and rubrics to honor creativity, as well as providing feedback around pushing creativity even further and deeper.

In my experiences where creativity has welcomed me in doctoral level courses, professors not only unlocked for me other possibilities, but also provided me with stipulations where I had to innovate and could not reinvent something which already exists for societal problems. When this occurred, it empowered me to dig into how I envision the possibility for the world. It is funny because it always begins with a picture before it is placed into words. These pictures that I speak of also have pushed me to start my own container to solve problems of our society which stifle the creativity of Black girls in a Black girl empowerment group I created, *Empowering Her Destiny*. In our organization, my goal is always to first help girls unpack and understand problems and issues that may exist around them, pushing against their ability to be free. From there, we dream up an ideal world where their talents and gifts have room to take up all the space possible. It is one of the only times that these girls have experienced, but I know if I show them how it feels once, they will always seek it.

GRETCHEN: REOPENING A PORTAL OF POSSIBILITY

What does it mean to be a conduit for Black Imaginations, to be charged with the guidance and care for Black doctoral students making their impact on our present and future world? During the COVID-19 pandemic, a portal temporarily opened to new possibilities and creative approaches to learning. As I was helping my own children navigate more open and free approaches to learning, I was simultaneously building new courses and experiences for HBCU graduate students. As a white woman committed to learning to build academic sanctuaries for Black students, I am privileged to witness Black doctoral students, their imaginations, and unique perspectives. This inquiry is about what they have taught and shown me about creativity and its possibility. The stakes are high and in many educational spaces, there is an instinct to push HBCU students to go harder, higher, and beyond expectations to prepare them for an inequitable, oppressive society. This can leave little room for imagination, dreaming, visioning, and creativity. After years of being witness to the process of Black doctoral students, I would argue that creativity and reimagining the future is central, not fanciful, superfluous, or a distraction. Creativity does not pull against rigor, expectations, and soaring outcomes but is rather central, rigorous work that graduate students should embody.

BLACK DOCTORAL STUDENTS AS GUIDES: STUDENT VIGNETTES

We asked Black doctoral students to answer questions about the role of creativity in their experiences in doctoral studies. The following four questions were used to guide their reflections or blurbs:

- What does creativity mean to you as a doctoral student? Define it in your own words.
- What role does creativity play for you as a doc student? Role of dreaming or visioning for the future?
- When has creativity been important or present in your experiences (coursework, assignments, research)?
- In an ideal world, what do you wish creativity could or should be for doctoral students or studies?

Ten Black doctoral students light the way, offering us stopping points via guiding questions. These guiding questions emerge from the following vignettes which offer a glimpse of their experiences with creativity in their doctoral journey.

Ariel: "More Nontraditional Methods and Less Rigidity"

As a doctoral student, I would define creativity as the opportunity to demonstrate knowledge and apply learning using nontraditional methods. It's hard to say because many courses have too much rigidity and don't allow for much creativity. Especially core courses. Unfortunately, I have had very limited opportunities in doctoral studies for creativity. Only in Dr. Y's classes and in a couple of Dr. Z's classes, I have been able to use my own creativity in crafting responses or presentations. I was able to co-produce a podcast as a culminating project once and we had a listening party. That was really inspiring and fun. In an ideal world, differentiated instruction would extend beyond K-12 learning environments and college students could be given the criteria that must be covered, but also the freedom to design their own activities to construct more meaningful experiences. No more cookie cutter posts with initial responses and then benign commentary on other people's posts.

Guide Qs: *How do we build opportunities for students to demonstrate knowledge and apply learning using nontraditional methods? How can our teaching or program be less rigid and more creative and inspiring?*

Victoria: 'Freedom of Choice and Voice'

Creativity as a doc student means having freedom of choice (text, product, etc) and freedom of voice (not discouraging interpretations of text, student voice shared in discussion—equal to teacher voice). It's a pretty important role in my studies as a doctoral student—the freedom to think critically on my own interpretations of text and especially in how I share those ideas. By allowing me to be as creative as I like, I get to dig deeper. Hindering that creativity encourages me to deliver whatever answers I assume the instructor is looking for and not my own. Creativity is not often encouraged in coursework/assignments and honestly I think this is due to utility and/or school or department culture. Having a lot of work to grade/old school instructing vs new school. One assignment that creativity was really encouraged was one where I was asked to design a course and draft a syllabus for it. It forced me to really think through my reading list for my dissertation and the themes that will emerge from them. Plus I was able to add things like a music playlist, TV shows, and podcasts related to themes/texts. I wish we were encouraged to include voices that may not be "scholarly" in our research—especially because so many women, Black and Indigenous voices have been left out of those "peer-reviewed" spaces. I wish there was more room for interdisciplinary engagement. I get it—one should be an expert on their topic, but we miss all the different angles we can study our topics from because interdisciplinary study is strongly encouraged within most doctoral programs. I also wish there was more flexibility in product. We write essays like that's the only way to convey a message. Especially when there are so many scholarly ways to communicate ideas—podcasts, vlogs, video essays, etc. I wish I could present my dissertation as a documentary but that's considered a creative dissertation and only allowed in creative writing despite it conveying the same ideas and scholarship in a way that can be shared beyond my committee. Like where do dissertations go to die after they've been defended?

    Guide Qs: *How do we give doc students freedom of voice and choice? In what ways are we hindering creative freedom instead of letting students dig deeper? How can we encourage voices who have been deemed outside of scholarly labels or spaces? How are we incorporating multimodal ways of knowing or showing learning? How will we offer more than a graveyard for dissertations?*

Candice: "Expanded Vision of myself as an expert and change agent"

In essence, as a doctoral student, creativity is not just about thinking outside the box; it's about redefining the box altogether and pushing the boundaries of knowledge in meaningful and innovative ways. Creativity has allowed me to see myself in many positions as an educational expert. Creativity has enabled me to see myself as a curriculum designer, crafting innovative learning experiences that cater to diverse learning styles and foster critical thinking, creativity, and lifelong learning skills. In another light, creativity has allowed me to see myself as a researcher, exploring cutting-edge theories and methodologies that push the boundaries of knowledge in education. Also, creativity has broadened my perspective on educational leadership, envisioning myself as a change agent who advocates for equity, inclusion, and social justice within educational institutions. In essence, creativity has expanded my vision of what it means to make a meaningful impact in the field of education. Creativity has been important to me in terms of original contribution to my field. Creativity enables me to generate original ideas or hypotheses that add value to the education literature and offer new insights into the phenomena I'm studying. For doctoral students, creativity should be purposeful when addressing meaningful research questions, solving real-world problems, and making substantial contributions to academia. Also, creativity should be open-minded. We should have an open-minded attitude toward exploring diverse perspectives, challenging conventional wisdom, and embracing uncertainty as we navigate the complexities of research. Lastly, creativity should be impactful. Creativity should be geared toward generating research outcomes that have a tangible impact, whether in academia, policymaking, or community engagement, contributing to positive change and societal progress.

Guide Qs: *How are we encouraging students to expand their vision of themselves as experts and change agents? How can creativity help our students explore diverse perspectives, challenge conventional wisdom and embrace uncertainty in their research?*

Davon: "Limitless possibilities"

Creativity, in my opinion, means having the freedom to include aspects of my identity in my work without any limits. I feel that there is no right or wrong regarding creativity as a doctoral student. I am the expert and should have free range to include what I please to prove my point or to get my point across. Returning to my definition, creativity plays a huge role as it allows me to think freely without any limitations. It allows me to express myself in a way that I feel I normally wouldn't be able to outside of the doctoral program. Obtaining my doctorate has always been a dream and to be doing the work now is truly amazing. I would say that creativity has been important in the assignments and research. I love doing projects and having the ability to create excites me. I am okay with having instructions for an assignment, however; I do not like feeling limited. Research is free range (once a topic is selected of course), however; the possibilities are limitless. I feel that creativity should be free range with no limits. It allows us doc students to be the very best versions of ourselves!

Guide Qs: *How can our program open up limitless possibilities for our students? How do we help them express themselves freely in ways they may not be able to outside of the program?*

Sabree: "Toil with the Possibilities"

Vision cannot exist without creative freedom. I think that as a doctoral student having the scholarly space to toil with the possibilities is important–it is a part of the learning experience. As a doctoral student, creativity means being encouraged to explore new ideas, especially as it relates to ways to defy what has always been done in American education to make it more equitable and applicable to the world around us. Creativity has been important for both coursework and research. Futurism was one of my favorite graduate courses because we were able to exercise a variety of mediums to convey our ideas. I urge all educational institutions to adopt creativity as a core value because the world is constantly evolving and over the past five years, we have been shown that anything is possible. Therefore, to sustain, there has to be space for creativity.

Guide Qs: How do we leverage creative freedom to support student visions? How can we carve out scholarly spaces to toil with possibilities? How do we encourage students to defy what has always been done and create a more equitable world? How can we adopt creativity as a core value to sustain the important work in our evolving world?

Marie-Gabrielle: "Collaboration- Thinking and Questions with Others"

To me creativity involves the capability to express ideas in a novel way in collaboration with others. As a doctoral student, creativity empowers and motivates me to be fully and actively present in cognitive activities with others by critically thinking and questioning ideas, beliefs, and my opinions in order to see and produce these ideas in a different way. In an ideal world, I wish creativity for doctoral students could include the following: (1) Have coursework that focuses more on dialog rather than lecture (2) Reduce coursework and focus more on courses that allow space for creativity, and (3) Have assignments that focus more on collaboration with the learning communities.

Creativity has been very important in my coursework and research that encouraged dialog with my peers and professors about world issues including the examination of the lived experiences of marginalized people, the causes and consequences of their experiences, and actions that could be taken to improve these experiences. Collaboration has contributed to my creativity by helping me to approach life issues with an open mind.

Guide Qs: How do we set up opportunities for doctoral students to collaborate that empowers them to question and build new approaches together? How can we anchor our learning communities to problem solving using lived experiences?

Cortnie: "Rid of the right(eous) way + Rooted in digging and planting anew"

As a doctoral student, creativity means taking up space to relate and respond to my research interests through self-expression. Sometimes creativity as a doc student looks like play. Sometimes it is saying or doing what has not been spoken but you feel. It is often divergent in your full praxis of thought, action, and reflection on text, intertextualities, intersectionalities, the dominant, the metaphysical, the metacognitive. This whole experience feels like a creative endeavor. Both as whatever medium or dimension or canvas employed to paint this vision and the acquired skill of how to get it all done, or leave it to find its way. There are times I am going for a walk immersed in a playlist, until my consciousness recenters on the reality that the creative is in conflict with the doc student's current experience. How dare I enjoy music when I could–should–need to be listening to a text? The vision for the future is a more creative syllabus. The vision for the future is to be rid of the right(eous) way. Creativity should not need to be called in as a great equalizer or resistance to dehumanization. Creativity is adaptability, belonging, process, and voice. It is a modeled practice for some while others wouldn't need an invitation, it is who they are.

> Moldy Ivory Towers.
> Thirty credits to discover.
> We real schooled. We
> be fooled. We
> rabbit research. We
> cyber church. We
> tick tock. We
> smear smocks. We
> power truth. We
> see you(th)*
>
> *Inspired by Gwendolyn Brooks, "We Real Cool"

We need creativity studios. We need to study effective programs that push beyond the normative gaze of the arts and those that simply sit as spectators. Does the time and economic infrastructure of a semester mirror the creative process? In an ideal world, we are not assigned, we collectively journey. I think creativity is like cultivating genius, as Muhammad (2020) states,

> History from Black communities tells us that educators don't need to empower youth or give them brilliance or genius. Instead, the power and genius is already within them, Genius is the brilliance, intellect, ability, cleverness, and artistry that have been flowing through their minds and spirits

across the generations. This cultivation calls for reaching back into the students' histories and deeply knowing them and their ancestries to teach in ways that raise, grow, and develop their existing genius. (p. 13)

We must be rooted in digging and planting anew.

Guide Qs: *How can we ensure our program is not a "moldy ivory tower" and leave room for play? How can we divest from the right(eous) ways and norms? How do we allow space for our students to "collectively journey" through their studies? How are we cultivating creativity that digs in and plants anew?*

Bobbi: "Breaking Barriers of Expertise + Think Passionately Beyond"

The doctoral degree in any discipline denotes those with authority who have contributed to their respective fields. These contributions require creativity: an intangible pathway to innovation, problem-solving, and, most importantly, learning. We are bound by the obligation to our work as educators, researchers, and community leaders to engage our creativity and the creativity of others as leaders in education. Creativity inspires us to think passionately about urban education; like sublime learning conditions, including how to make the world ours and our students' classroom. At the same time, creativity for doctoral students breaks the barrier between the doctoral student and their students, colleagues, and staff who regard them as the sole community "expert." It pushes into the universe of collaboration, moving from exercising power to sharing power. Creativity for the doctoral student lets us see learning beyond standardized testing, and exclusionary discipline practices, all while wrapping us up in the most encouraging and inspiring conditions to break beyond the status quo and build anew.

Guide Qs: *How are we breaking barriers of expertise and sharing power? How are we wrapping doc students in encouraging and inspiring conditions? How do we push students to break beyond the* status quo *and build anew?*

Tami: "Identifying Unheard of Possibilities to Combat Problems"

As a doctoral student, creativity means to take an innovative approach to the work. There is tons of research out there, so creativity and innovative thinking is required. Asking new questions and identifying unheard of possibilities to combat problems in our area of focus. We have to consider what hasn't been said, ask new questions and explore the unconventional.

The role of creativity is important as we draft innovative research methodologies or integrate multiple disciplines to explore a research problem from different angles and address gaps in existing literature through creative thinking. It shows up in challenging conventional wisdom and critically evaluating existing theories and paradigms to uncover new insights and ensuring that we effectively communicate complex ideas and findings in creative and engaging ways, whether through academic papers, presentations, or other mediums as we did in Dr. X's courses.

Creativity for a doctoral student is about being intellectually adventurous and willing to explore uncharted territories in pursuit of knowledge and understanding.

Guide Qs: *How do we provide space and opportunity for doctoral students to be intellectually adventurous, to challenge prior research? What are the uncharted territories in research? How do we elevate new research ideas and differing research products as part of the work instead of other than or outside of the work?*

Brittney: "Reimagining New Solutions to Old Problems"

As a doctoral student, creativity means that I have the space and opportunity to explore my research interests. Creativity allows for doctoral students to be able to reimagine new solutions to old problems. it also allows for there to be a counternarratives at the center of research.

Creativity was present when I took Dr. X's Futurism class. In this course, I had the opportunity to explore a variety of pathways to analyze problems and new solutions. In an ideal world, creativity should be the center of all of the work for doctoral students and studies. Being able to reimagine systems, studies, and protocols allows for there to be solutions. The process of creativity is also a form of decolonization.

Guide Qs: *How do we center creativity in doctoral work? What are the opportunities that students are afforded to choose how they work or what their work products will be? What is the difference in some classes that in others that sparks creativity?*

GUIDES FROM ACROSS GALAXIES: BLACK CREATIVES

Although Black doctoral students serve as our innermost guides to reimagining creativity in doctoral studies, we also call on guides orbiting across galaxies: foundational Black scholars, educators, researchers, and artists. We lean on the wisdom of artists Alma Thomas, Zora Neale Hurston, and Simone Leigh, the refusal work named by Jasmine Mahmoud, the critical review of Dr. Lori Patton Davos and colleagues, and the foundational framings of Ruha Benjamin. They reveal that the role of creativity can be an affirmation of Black humanity and legacy, a work of refusal of limitations, a practice of self-care that should expand to institutional care, an unapologetically Black experience that is central to student success at HBCUs, and ultimately, a docking station to a freer future.

Creativity Affirms Humanity: an "Ancient Reckoning"

> *Through color, I have sought to concentrate on beauty and happiness, rather than on man's inhumanity to man…I've never bothered painting the ugly things in life. People struggling, having difficulty. You meet that when you go out, and then you have to come back and see the same thing hanging on the wall. No. I wanted something beautiful that you could sit down and look at. And then, the paintings change you.* Alma Thomas (1891–1978)

Educator and artist Alma Thomas found sanctuary in her creative process. She saw creative expression as a way to affirm her humanity in the midst of a tumultuous battle for civil rights. She was the vanguard for interracial artist spaces, and she dedicated the majority of her life to teaching art to Black students in Washington D.C. She describes creativity as a way to affirm her humanity in the midst of ongoing dehumanization. She also reminds us of the potential for creativity and artistic expression to be catalysts for change. Through her life and her art, Thomas models creativity as an immersive, vital, necessary, and humanizing process.

Guide Qs: *How do we humanize our processes and programs? How do we infuse our programs with beauty and joy? How will we channel creativity as a protective layer against dehumanization? How do we inspire each other to create in a way that transforms?*

Creatives, through their natural gifts and authenticity, make things happen in the world, uniting people for all sorts of purposes. Wherever they are in time, people have beautiful artistic gifts within them. They share their gifts with the world to connect people and connect with people, to raise awareness, to spur people into action, to fight back, to celebrate. Creatives are all really important and they don't have to look the same to get our attention. In fact, the fact that they are different is why we pay attention. The difference shakes us up a bit. It captures us uniquely starting with our senses, working its way into our heart, and then pushing to the consciousness of our mind. Creativity can be a vehicle that taps into the wealth of past and present Black artists, thinkers, educators, and activists. A space to dream is intimately bound with the wealth of Black humanity. The recently departed artist Faith Ringgold once said, "My ideas come from reflecting on my life and the lives of people I have known and have been in some way inspired by." Ringgold's creativity is innately tied to those whom she knows and have inspired her.

Guide Qs: *How do we design or redesign graduate education to allow space for self reflection, and the wisdom and solutions found in the lives of students' ancestors?*

Zora Neale Hurston (2002) is another foundational expert on the legacy of Black creativity and expression. In her essay "The Characteristics of Negro Expression," Zora Neale Hurston distills the "will to adorn" which "does not attempt to meet conventional standards, but it satisfies the soul of its creator." Hurston reminds us that Black expression will not align with conventions and standards, and instead is akin to soul work. She also insists that "no little moment passes unadorned" is tied to Black expression's "desire for beauty...The feeling...that there can never be enough of beauty, let alone too much." Most people would not overlap the notion of adornment or beauty with graduate studies, but the idea of making room for beauty of thought, beauty of discussion, and beauty of design of new frameworks is worth considering. Another important part of expression according to Hurston is originality which she names as asymmetry in response to "the abrupt and unexpected changes." Her analysis is that the response to unexpected changes is "but easily workable" for a Black student "accustomed to the break in going from one part to another, so that he adjusts himself to the new tempo." Hurston urges us to see the beauty in originality and ability to adjust beautifully to unexpected shifts.

Guide Qs: *Are institutions or individuals ready to rethink conventions and standards and incorporate soul work? How can we make space for beautiful originality and strengths of redirection? What original adjustments do we need to make to our programs?*

Sculptor Simone Leigh illuminates the importance of claiming your audience and the importance of change in creativity. In an interview, Leigh describes her creative process: "A destiny to change and adapt seems the perfect metaphor to describe my...ongoing exploration of black female subjectivity. I am charting a history of change and adaptation through objects and gesture and the unstoppable forward movement of black women." Leigh's creative declaration inspires us to rethink how we embed the 'destiny to change and adapt' in our programs and courses, as well as how we design for the "unstoppable forward movement of black women" and students in our care. Leigh's artistic creations have been described as "an ancient reckoning with the elements" (Rhodes-Pitts, 2019) which also serves as a guide to rethinking creativity in doctoral courses.

Guide Qs: *Do students walk away tapped into or feeling part of the "unstoppable forward movement?" And how can we connect them to their legacy, and destiny to adapt and change their world/s? Do our courses offer students an "ancient reckoning" with academic ancestors and predecessors? Do we prepare ourselves and our students for such a reckoning and build for what waits on the other side of that creative process?*

Creativity as a Work of Refusal on Limitations

Creativity has also been described as a "work of refusal" of limitations. Jasmine Mahmoud reported on a Tacoma Art Museum event entitled *How We See Us: On the Refusal of Limitations on Black Creativity* talking about the "long genealogy of Black artists and administrators doing this work of refusal" (Mahmoud, 2022). The refusal of limitations on what Black artists or scholars should be involves "double work of expression and anti-racism" or pushing back against the limitations or "containers" put on Black scholars (Mahmoud, 2022). One part of the refusal is the limits on what being a doctoral student means, especially related to beliefs about identity. According to artist Faith Ringgold (2024), "After I decided to be an artist, the first thing that I had to believe was that I, a Black woman, could be on the art scene without sacrificing one iota of my blackness, or my femaleness, or my humanity" ("Faith Ringgold"). In her creativity, Ringgold refuses a fractured identity and dehumanization.

Guide Qs: *How do we ensure that Black doctoral students are welcomed and encouraged to integrate all parts of their identity so as not to be sacrificed in the quest for a doctoral degree? Are students free to "decide" to be a doc student with creativity and identity intact? Does our program invite a refusal of dehumanization?*

Unapologetically BCEE for Grad Students

A new study done on undergraduates at HBCUs named what they call "unapologetically Black creative educational experiences" (Patton et al., 2022). This study focused on Black Creative Educational Experiences (BCEE) as essential ingredients to undergraduate Black students at HBCUs thriving and succeeding. This ground-breaking critical review offers a definition of BCEE as "participatory, performative cultural experiences created by or for students, centering Black artistic expression, aesthetics, and engagement" such as "choirs, marching bands, dance teams, and spoken word poetry" (Patton et al., 2022). Many of the experiences studied are not a central part of the graduate experience at an HBCU, which begs the question, what are the "unapologetically Black creative educational experiences" for doctoral students? A central part of the study is the "methodological guide...centering Black ways of knowing" (Patton et al., 2022) that is informed by Boutte et al.'s (2017) Legacies and Dimensions of African Culture (LDAC). Three of the eleven listed LDAC really resonate with the study of creativity in doctoral studies: communalism/collectively, expressive individualism, and improvisation:

> *Communalism/collectively*—a commitment to social connectedness, which includes an awareness that social bonds and responsibilities transcend individual privilege

Expressive individualism—the cultivation of a distinctive personality and proclivity for spontaneous and genuine personal expression

Improvisation—substitution of alternatives that are more sensitive to Black culture. (Boutte et al., 2017, pp. 70–711)

This research "acknowledge[s] the influence of Black creative expression on research and practice...viewing Black creative expression as knowledge production" (Patton et al., 2022, p. 64). What makes BCEEs so important for Black student success is that they are "rooted in intellectual and expressive freedom...and community building" (64). As part of "Black mattering in education research" (p. 66) as well as high impact practices, researchers argue that BCEE should be a central focus and priority in higher education.

Guide Qs: *What are unapologetically BCCEE for doctoral students at HBCUs? How is "intellectual and expressive freedom" built into our program?*

Creativity as a Docking Station to a Freer Future

"They enact ways of building worlds and being in the world" ~ Simone Leigh (Sharifa Rhodes-Pitts, 2019)

In the words of artist Simone Leigh, creativity is akin to world building, and as the subheading suggests, a docking station to a freer future. Ruha Benjamin in her latest book *Imagination: A Manifesto* shares her "idea of a collective imagination, as when we imagine different worlds together, writing shared stories and plotting futures in which we can all flourish" (Benjamin, x). She urges us to "learn to protect our imaginations" because they hold such power which is why "those in power work tirelessly to squash us from having radical imaginations that dare to envision a world in which everyone can thrive" (x). She invites us to "exorcis[e] our mental and social structures from the tyranny of dominant imaginaries" and writes an inspiring "field guide for seeding an imagination grounded in solidarity" (8). She offers a clear blueprint for creativity in doctoral studies from her own pedagogy and practice:

> I draw upon over a decade of teaching that aims to build students' powers of speculation with projects that involve imagining tools, toolkits, and worlds that break with current social hierarchies. In the process, we will confront the little voice in our head whose job it has been to police our own imagination... We need to give the voice of the cynical, skeptical grouch that patrols the borders of our imagination a rest...Imagination is a field of struggle, not an ephemeral afterthought that we have the luxury to dismiss or romanticize. (p. 8)

Guide Qs: *How do we design a program that is a docking station to a freer future? What imagining tools and toolkits will we need to break with current social hierarchies? How will we guide students through imagination as a field of struggle and site to plot a different future? How will our work seed imaginations grounded in solidarity?*

From Self-Care to Institutional Care

During the COVID pandemic, culture and community organizations surveyed people about their connections to community organizations. Their final report names creativity as a core value, categorizing creativity and self-care as personal practices (Buyukozer et al., 2021). But what if institutions embedded creativity as an institutional practice? And what would that look like for Black doctoral students? If creativity is seen as a tool for self-care as well as connection with others as well, then "sparking collective change" would mean a "radical reimagining" (Buyukozer et al., 2021, p. 12). Even though the report focused on culture-and-community organizations, the findings can be applied to higher education institutions as well, especially the role of creativity. The findings show:

> ...that creativity is an inherent part of being human. But while people don't need help being creative...organizations...may be missing opportunities to validate and celebrate community members' creative actions or to connect them with others who enjoy similar kinds of creativity...In many cases, personal creativity is linked closely to self-care, connection (in multiple senses), and overall well-being. And there's a wide spectrum of creativity already in play. (Buyukozer et al., 2021, p. 6)

Applied to colleges and universities, the question becomes, how are higher education institutions missing similar opportunities to "validate and celebrate" students' creativity and capitalize on the relationship between creativity, connection and well-being for students? The study's findings also indicate a direct link between self-care practices, personal creativity and spaces "of collective processing to support mental, physical, and communal well-being" (p. 7). In the section on "Rethinking Creativity," the report reminds us that creativity can facilitate connection "with ourselves and our heritage and identities, and with our pasts and futures" which ultimately "can contribute to a more fundamental one: greater well-being at both an individual and collective level" (p. 11). Part of the radical reimagining process is the value we place on creators, reframing them "as visionaries: possibility-seers, divergent thinkers, imaginers, reframers, and do-ers who are integral to social change and healthy communities" (p. 11). This is a widening and amplification process: "This would include valuing Black artists and creatives and embracing their innovations by widening the definitions of existing fields and genres to amplify them" (Buyukozer et al., 2021, p. 11). Amplifying innovation and reframing students as visionaries and change agents is central to cultivating institutional care.

Guide Qs: *Is it foreseeable that institutions will value creativity as a process of care for individuals and communities? How can universities widen and amplify the role and gifts of Black creatives in their institutions?*

RADICAL REIMAGININGS AND POSSIBILITIES

In the chapter called "Imagining the Future," Ruha Benjamin reminds us that "creative works can spark counterimaginaries that have the potential to dream bigger and materialize into concrete changes" (Benjamin, 2024, p. 99), and she also reminds us that "our theories are the first draft of reality. And the stories we tell (about) ourselves lay the groundwork for the kind of world we then create to sustain the people we are imaged to be" (Benjamin, 2024, p. 105). Benjamin offers exercises for what she calls an "imagination incubator." In our process to radically reimagine what creativity should be for doctoral studies, we continue to ask ourselves and our institutions, how are we incubators for a freer future?

Jacque: Reimagining Research and Refusing THIS BOX

I was taught that research was not creative. I was taught not to use personal language, and that there was no room for personal stories or creativity. As a creative, this caused me to shy away from research. I found the way it was taught, the process, and the products to be boring. I am a writer. I love words and stories. To not use beautiful words eloquently in a paper was almost painful. I felt boxed in. The box didn't work for me. I did enough to get by but just enough.

If you are a person of color and used to expressing yourself in a certain way, The Box may not work for you. When I found myself on my doctoral journey, I had to remember that I had a professor before that told me that stories were research — this only happened in graduate school one time — striking that this did not happen again until now in my doctoral journey. I went to two PWIs, so I was boxed in for college. I was told that these are the ways that you do academic writing/research. I was limited to producing research papers. When I was lucky, I may be able to throw in a presentation here and there.

Even with creative writing, there are certain things I could not write about. The topics were dry. They did not speak to Black people. Most often when I proposed a research topic, I was told that it was not appropriate for research or that it was too provocative. The elements of Whiteness that were always present was the way of knowing and not knowing each other. The measurable ways of knowing people were the acceptable ones to write about. You cannot measure one's heart, soul, pain, and struggle. Those were the things that I was discouraged from researching. White culture determines what is normal. This extends to what and how we research. Having the experience of attending both PWIs and now an HBCU, I know that those norms do not apply to the oasis of the HBCU, or more accurately, they do not have to. When you do the work of research you can create your own process and products. I imagine a world where the chains are broken for every doctoral student who wants to create through their research. It is fully possible.

Final Dispatch Recommendations

Because we now view creativity as a docking station to a freer future, we learn and lead with an orientation to this truth. We ventured on creative dispatches in two senses of the word. In one sense, a creative dispatch is the sending of a person to a place for a purpose, and that purpose is to create a new future. In another sense, these dispatches serve as official reports from the field of doctoral studies. Our advice for educators and doctoral students who may be considering creative dispatching, is first and foremost, group travel is highly recommended. Even for times when you find yourself alone, dispatched to the field, you still need your base team to stay in contact with. Creativity as a group activity is grounding and sustaining, even in difficult times. We found that creativity ignites sparks that are contagious, and really lead to on-going, transformative learning for the group. We also caution against compromising on creativity. Some people argue that creativity needs structures or some constraints in order to thrive, but our journey has taught us that creativity invites more openness, flexibility, and space to dream up unlimited, endless possibilities for the future of ourselves and our world. Like Alma Thomas, we urge you to literally reach for the moon, dreaming and constructing new galaxies and systems.

In conclusion, our Black doctoral guides offer a clear framework with specific guidelines. Their insights answer three main questions about creativity in doctoral studies: with whom, how or with what, and for what purpose.

With whom?

>   Collaboration is central
>   Space to think and question with others
>   Breaking barriers of expertise
>   An expanded vision of myself as an expert

How, or with what?

>   Getting rid of the right(eous) way
>   With freedom of choice and voice
>   Toiling with limitless possibilities in mind
>   Thinking passionately beyond

For what purpose?

An expanded vision of myself as a change agent
Identifying unheard of possibilities to combat problems
Reimagining new solutions to old problems
Rooted in digging and planting anew

Building and co-creating transformative learning spaces in doctoral programs has a long-lasting impact on professors, students, and their communities. It is worth the journey to places unknown or unfamiliar, and worth the risk to interrupt internalized and externalized status quo and norms. As Ruha Benjamin invokes, imagination is a manifesto, and we must clearly demand creativity in doctoral studies as a nonnegotiable future we create together.

REFERENCES

Benjamin, R. (2024). *Imagination: A manifesto*. Norton.
Boutte, G., Johnson, G. L., Wynter-Hoyte, K., & Uyoata, U. E. (2017). Using African diaspora literacy to heal and restore the souls of young black children. *International critical childhood policy studies journal, 6*(1), 66–79.
Buyukozer, M. D., Knight, C. K., Treptow, T., & Guerrero, C. (2021, November). *A place to be heard: Black perspectives on creativity, trustworthiness, welcome and well-being——findings from a qualitative study*. Slover-Linett.
Hurston, Z. N. (2002). *Characteristics of Negro expression (1934)* (pp. 24–31). Negro: An Anthology.
Mahmoud, J. (2022, April 18). Three lessons from 'How we see us: On the refusal of limitations on Black creativity. *Tacoma Art Museum*. https://www.tacomaartmuseum.org/tamblog-current-three-lessons/
Muhammad, G. (2020). *Cultivating genius: An equity framework for culturally and historically responsive literacy*. Scholastic Incorporated.
Patton, L. D., Jenkins, T. S., Howell, G. L., & Keith Jr, A. R. (2022). Unapologetically black creative educational experiences in higher education: A critical review. *Review of Research in Education, 46*(1), 64–104.
Rhodes-Pitts, S. (2019). *Simone Leigh: For her own pleasure and edification*. The Hugo Boss Prize 2018. The Guggenheim Museums and Foundation.
Ringgold, F. (2024). *The art story of Faith Ringgold*. The Art Story Foundation. https://www.theartstory.org/artist/ringgold-faith/
Thomas, A. (1978). *American art*. Smithsonian Institute. https://americanart.si.edu/artist/alma-thomas-4778

ADDITIONAL READING

Prize 2018. *The Guggenheim Museums and foundation*.
Rhodes-Pitts, S. (2019). *Simone Leigh: For her own pleasure and edification*. The Hugo Boss Prize 2018. The Guggenheim Museums and Foundation.

SECTION 3

FLEXIBILITY AND ADAPTABILITY IN HIGHER EDUCATION

CHAPTER 7

INTERNATIONALIZATION OF HIGHER EDUCATION: INTERNATIONAL STUDENTS' PERSPECTIVES

Merab Mushfiq
York University, Canada

ABSTRACT

The enrollment of international students in higher education has grown significantly worldwide, bringing both opportunities and challenges. These students often face obstacles such as language barriers, academic difficulties, cultural adjustment, and limited engagement. As a result, there is an increasing need to internationalize teaching and curriculum to foster a greater sense of belonging for international students while also equipping all students—domestic and international—with the intercultural competencies necessary to thrive in a global society. Internationalizing the curriculum enhances inclusivity and prepares students to become global citizens by developing their cultural awareness, communication skills, and global perspectives. This approach not only supports international students' academic and social success but also enriches the learning experience for all students. This chapter explores effective strategies for internationalizing teaching and curriculum, drawing from both faculty perspectives and student experiences. It examines how inclusive pedagogical practices and culturally responsive content can create more engaging, equitable, and globally informed classrooms. By incorporating diverse voices and worldviews into course design and delivery, educators can better address the needs of international students and promote intercultural learning across the academic community.

Keywords: International students; curriculum internationalization; higher; education; intercultural competence; inclusive teaching strategies

After spending more than a decade in higher education and working across various departments—including faculty, academic affairs, student affairs, and support services—I have had the opportunity to work with diverse range of students from various backgrounds. As a former international student and working in higher education has given me an opportunity to bring my own lived experiences as well as collective experiences of my students, including international students. While most of the focus has been given to international students' academic challenges and transitioning into their host institution, there is limited research available on institutional support, competent staff and faculty members that would support international and local students by bringing the international education components into their teaching and practices in higher education using student voice. Students' voices, let alone international students' voices, have been largely absent from the current discussion of internationalization of higher education (Sung et al., 2024). In this chapter, I am highlighting my own voice as a former international student, faculty member, student affairs professional and my students' voices who I had the pleasure of working with in the last ten years. My focus is on discussing strategies and practices that are beneficial for international students from their perspectives and from my own lived experiences.

International students add a unique and rich "diversity of identities, cultures, languages and world views to the learning environment, adding a global dimension" (University of Calgary, 2020, p. 9) to their hosts' institutions and host countries. The number of international students has been continuously increasing in higher education institutions around the globe. Many countries and institutions especially in North America rely on international student enrollment as a way to generate revenue and bolster their economies (Banks & Bhandari, 2012). In 2023, when I was teaching in a community college in North America, 90% of my students were international students in one course and about 95% in another. There are many challenges that these students face such as academic difficulties, language barriers, acculturative stress, financial burdens, finding employment on- and/or off-campus, and social network to name a few (Mushfiq, 2023). Integrating into a host country and host institutions' environment needs support from faculty, staff members, peers, and community members. While these students face many challenges transitioning into a new culture, most of them also face academic challenges. Academic writing (Elliot et al., 2016), language barriers hinder communication and interaction with peers and faculty members (Yu & Wright, 2017), which in turn affects students' well-being and academic success (Sato & Este, 2018).

My students were continuously having challenges of transitioning into a new education system, participating during class discussions and teamwork was a new concept for many of them. Because of language barriers and communication challenges, my students had a hard time understanding and completing assignments on time. In order to meet the needs of my students, I had to revise my teaching strategies and assessments. I not only incorporated international education components into my course content but also actively sought opportunities to support all of my students in meaningful ways. One strategy involved allowing students to choose a topic related to their favorite cultural festival or a historical event, which they were then asked to design, facilitate, and present to their peers. Although they followed specific prompts provided to them, the opportunity to select a personally meaningful festival or event significantly increased their motivation. All students were actively engaged during the lecture and presentations. Some brought traditional food to share, others wore cultural attire, and some shared family photographs and music associated with their festival. This activity encouraged students to interact with each other and led to an increase in class discussions and engagement from that point forward during class.

APPROACHES OF INTERNATIONALIZATION

While there is no universal or a standard definition of internationalization, it is commonly conceptualized as the process of incorporating international and intercultural dimensions within higher education practices and learning spaces (Knight, 2003). De Wit (2002) further added that "multicultural education, intercultural education, cross-cultural education, education for international understanding, peace education, global education, transnational studies, and global studies" (p. 103) should be incorporated to advance internationalization approaches and practices in higher education. Furthermore, Internationalization at home is more curriculum-orientated and focuses on activities that develop international or global understanding and intercultural skills" (de Wit et al., 2015, p. 45). This form of internationalization refers to "the purposeful integration of international and intercultural dimensions into the formal and informal curriculum for all students within domestic learning environments" (Beelen & Jones, 2015, p. 76). Creating an environment to encourage building relationships with international students, respecting each other in the classroom, and encouraging international students to participate by learning about each other's cultures (King & Bailey, 2021).

Over the past ten years, I have been committed to fostering and promoting social change that generates meaningful impact both locally and globally. Creating a safe and inclusive classroom environment is essential to me, as it allows for open and respectful discussions and dialogues. I strive to cultivate this space by inviting diverse guest speakers to enrich classroom discussions, providing students with opportunities to express their thoughts in a respectful way. These practices are crucial for fostering mutual understanding and encouraging students to engage with diverse perspectives.

It is important to create a space to campus community and especially to students as a means of empowering their identities and equipped them with skills and awareness of themselves, and the society that we live in, and of the world as well (Simm & Marvell, 2017). It is necessary to have programming that provides international and cross-cultural perceptions and awareness to students (Hayward & Siaya, 2001) through curriculum and support services that have international components to enhance student engagement, success and learning experiences. I have served on various committees and organized cultural events such as the International Festival, Home Away From Home, and Cultural Day. I was involved in planning and actively participated in activities including international music processions, flag ceremonies, sharing of ethnic cuisines, traditional attire, and cultural performances. These events provided meaningful opportunities for both local and international students—as well as the wider campus community—to come together to celebrate local and global cultures and promote on-campus diversity. Such initiatives fostered a sense of belonging among all students but more specifically—international students, offering them a space to interact with peers, build friendships, and expand their social networks. Events like these were valuable for the campus community and helped in increasing awareness of the diverse cultural backgrounds and values students contribute to the campus environment.

APPROACHES OF INTERNATIONALIZATION

International Students' Perspectives

It is well documented that many international students face language barriers, and sometimes due to limited English-language proficiency can restrict interaction between international and domestic students (Arkoudis et al., 2019). This often hinders their participation in class and reduces their overall engagement on campus. Therefore, there is a pressing need to enhance students' experiences by implementing initiatives and programs that focus on developing communication skills, as well as fostering intercultural understanding and awareness. As a staff member working in the international department at a small university where the number of international students were increasing every year, I realized that students were struggling in many different ways and they were not sure about how to overcome those challenges and barriers. After observing and speaking with students, I realized that there were no structured programs in place to facilitate interaction between international and domestic students. Many international students lacked friendships with their peers and were unaware of available resources for them on-campus for academic success and support. To better understand their needs, I conducted informal one-on-one conversations and small group discussions. In response, I collaborated with various departments and implemented multiple initiatives aimed at fostering inclusion and improving access to support services and navigating academic practices and learning.

COFFEE HOURS

Introduced "Coffee Hours" as an informal program where international students could learn about the host culture through interactions with domestic students, faculty and staff, and community members. Initially implemented as a pilot program for one semester but because the program received a huge positive feedback and as a result this program was subsequently continued. Over time, it evolved into a welcoming space for all participants to connect, share experiences, and learn about diverse cultures and histories.

Peer Mentoring

Many international students experience acculturative stress when they first arrive on campus (Elliot et al., 2016; Mushfiq, 2023), and having a mentor or structured mentoring program in place can significantly support their transition. Regular interaction with peer mentors—especially those trained in intercultural competencies and communication—can help international students navigate both academic and social environments. Matching mentors with mentees who share similar backgrounds or interests can foster confidence and contribute to students' academic and emotional well-being (Lorenzetti et al., 2023). Peer mentors can also guide students through co-curricular activities, job search strategies, and academic challenges, offer diverse perspectives, and help them build a social network.

At my previous institution, I served on a peer mentoring committee that introduced a program in which students were matched with mentors based on shared interests and goals. Mentors were required to complete various training sessions which helped them to be prepared to effectively support their mentees. They were also equipped with tools and resources to guide their mentoring efforts. Regular check-ins with both mentors and mentees were conducted by staff to identify and address any gaps in support.

Tutoring Support

In addition to acculturative stress, academic difficulties such as academic writing, comprehension of course material and assignments, different styles and varieties of assessments, and proper citations are significant challenges that many international students face. Certainly, I experienced some of these challenges myself, despite having strong communication skills. As a faculty member, I have noticed many of my students struggle with academic tasks such as writing, critical thinking, comprehension, and articulating ideas in a professional manner. To address these issues, I collaborated with the tutoring center and the international student department to create dedicated tutoring support hours specifically designed for international students. These sessions aimed to help them overcome writing challenges and other academic obstacles. Students were encouraged to attend and ask questions in a supportive environment. In addition, weekly drop-in hours were established to offer targeted assistance in writing skills.

FACULTY SUPPORT AND UNDERSTANDING

Faculty plays a very important role in student learning, growth, understanding, and overall student development. International students usually do not participate in the classroom especially in the initial years due to their language barriers, low confidence level, and also because they feel like an outsider (O'Dea, 2023). Due to language barrier, cultural differences, and communication expectations in host country creates a stressful situation for many international students. Most students are not aware of resources and student support services that are available for them to utilize because the concept of student support services is new to them (Martirosyan et al., 2019). International students need faculty support in many different as they rely heavily on faculty members. As a faculty member, I consistently sought out campus resources to support international students and guided them on how to access these services—for example, how to schedule an appointment at the tutoring center, where the centers are located, how to connect with academic advising, and where to find the campus food bank and other essential support services. It is important for faculty to be aware of the various resources and support systems available to students on campus. Collaboration between faculty and student support services is essential, as students often develop long-term relationships with their instructors through regular classroom interaction. Inviting guest speakers for classroom discussions has encouraged greater student participation and engagement. Additionally, inviting staff from various student services to present in class has been beneficial, helping students connect with on-campus resources and increasing their awareness of available support.

My students were more engaged and attentive in the classroom when they observed a diversity of guest speakers and various student support staff members came during the lectures. They became even more invested when they realized their assignments welcomed the inclusion of their own cultural values, festivals, food, language, and music. Students not only presented topics that were personally meaningful to them, but also learned from one another by sharing their unique cultural perspectives. This approach created opportunities for all students to engage, connect, and develop intercultural understanding. Student evaluations clearly reflected their appreciation for these experiences, highlighting the value of learning about diversity, different cultures, and the rich backgrounds each student contributed to the environment of the classroom and the shared learning space that we all created.

CONCLUSION

Incorporating the voices of international students in the internationalization of higher education is essential, as these students contribute unique perspectives, experiences, and cultural insights. Their participation enhances community building, fosters cultural awareness, and promotes respect for diverse cultures and viewpoints within both the classroom and the broader campus community. This transnational and cross-culture learning experience within and beyond campus promotes global awareness and cross-cultural skills (Sung et al., 2024). These initiatives served an important purpose to the higher education institutions where I have served in various different roles to promote, engage, and design cocurricular activities and curriculum that support cross-cultural communication, awareness, and competency.

Integrating international components into teaching practices and within other areas of higher education can be achieved through the inclusion of global perspectives and international issues within course modules, the promotion of intercultural dialogue, and the development of socially responsible global citizenship and empathy for others in diverse environments and societies (Simm & Marvell, 2017). International students are more likely to engage with course content, faculty, and peers when they are given opportunities to represent their cultures, values, and perspectives, or to discuss current issues and trends relevant to their backgrounds. These opportunities also create space for all students to learn about intercultural communication, cultural humility, and to broaden their understanding of global perspectives.

There is a growing need to internationalize all sectors of higher education—including teaching, academic practices, student support services, and staff development. In today's interconnected world, students must learn to understand global issues, appreciate diverse viewpoints, and cultivate patience, humility, and empathy as global citizens. Within higher education, it is important to embed international components in curricula, teaching practices, and support services fosters a greater sense of belonging and encourages active participation in class and campus life. Such exposure helps develop cultural humility, sensitivity, and intercultural competence in students within higher education.

Incorporating student voices, especially international students, is essential when implementing changes aimed at improving student outcomes and advancing higher education. International students are a valuable asset to higher education institutions, bringing diverse perspectives, experiences, and global awareness to the academic community and to support them effectively, both faculty and support staff must receive ongoing, targeted training and professional development. Faculty need to be equipped with the tools and strategies necessary to foster inclusive and culturally responsive classrooms. Likewise, support staff require access to resources and strategic implementation plans to embed international components into their daily practices. These efforts benefit the entire student body but are particularly impactful for international students, as implementation of such programming and activities promote a sense of belonging. When international students feel included and supported, they are better able to navigate challenges, cope with acculturative stress, and succeed both academically and socially.

REFERENCES

Arkoudis, S., Dollinger, M., Baik, C., & Patience, A. (2019). International students' experience in Australian higher education: Can we do better? *Higher Education, 77*(5), 799–813. https://doi.org/10.1007/s10734-018-0302-x

Banks, M., & Bhandari, R. (2012). Global student mobility. In D. K. Deardorff, H. de Wit, J. D. Heyl, & T. Adams (Eds.), *The SAGE handbook of international higher education* (pp. 379–398). SAGE Publications, Incorporated. https://doi.org/10.4135/9781452218397.n21

De Wit, H. (2002). *Internationalization of higher education in the United States of America and Europe: A historical, comparative and conceptual analysis*. Greenwood Press.

Elliot, D. L., Reid, K., & Baumfield, V. (2016). Beyond the amusement, puzzlement and challenges: An enquir y into international students' academic acculturation. *Studies in Higher Education, 41*(12), 2198–2217. https://doi.org/10.1080/03075079.2015.1029903

Hayward, F., & Siaya, L. M. (2001). *Public experience, attitudes, and knowledge: A report on two national surveys about international education* (Vol. 1, p. 67).

King, C. S. T., & Bailey, K. S. (2021). Intercultural communication and US higher education: How US students and faculty can improve: International students' classroom experiences. *International Journal of Intercultural Relations, 82*(Complete), 278–287. https://doi.org/10.1016/j.ijintrel.2021.04.007

Knight, J. (2003). Updating the definition of internationalization. *International Higher Education*, (33), 2–3.

Lorenzetti, D. L., Lorenzetti, L., Nowell, L., Jacobsen, M., Clancy, T., Freeman, G., & Paolucci, E. O. (2023). Exploring international graduate students' experiences, challenges, and peer relationships: Impacts on academic and emotional well-being. *Journal of International Students*, *13*(4), 22–41. https://doi.org/10.32674/jis.v14i2.5186

Martirosyan, N. M., Bustamante, R. M., & Saxon, D. P. (2019). Academic and social support services for international students: Current practices. *Journal of International Students*, *21*(1), 172–191. https://doi.org/10.32674/jis.v9i1.275

Mushfiq, M. (2023). International student transition to Canadian post-secondary institutions. *Comparative & International Higher Education*, *15*(4), 96–105. https://doi.org/10.32674/jcihe.v15i4.4921

O'Dea, X. (2023). Enhancing a sense of academic and social belongingness of Chinese direct-entry students in the post-covid era: A UK context. *Perspectives: Policy and Practice in Higher Education*, *28*(2), 97–108. https://doi.org/10.1080/13603108.2023.2255838

Sato, C., & Este, D. (2018). From multiculturalism to critical multiculturalism. In D. Este, L. Lorenzetti, & C. Sato (Eds.), *Racism and anti-racism in Canada* (pp. 329–366). Fernwood Publishing.

Simm, D., & Marvell, A. (2017). Creating global students: Opportunities, challenges and experiences of internationalizing the geography curriculum in higher education. *Journal of Geography in Higher Education*, *41*(4), 467–474. https://doi.org/10.1080/03098265.2017.1373332

Sung, M. C., Wang, Y., & Vong, K. I. P. (2024). Multiple voices and multiple interests: Students' lived experiences and understanding of university internationalization. *Asia Pacific Educ. Rev.* https://doi.org/10.1007/s12564-024-09947-4

University of Calgary. (2020). *Global engagement plan 2020 - 2025*.

Yu, B., & Wright, E. (2017). Academic adaptation amid internationalisation: The challenges for local, mainland Chinese, and international students at Hong Kong's universities. *Tertiary Education and Management*, *23*(4), 347–360. https://doi.org/10.1080/13583883.2017.1356365

ADDITIONAL READING

Elkin, G., Devjee, F. & Farnsworth, J. (2005). Visualising the "internationalisation" of universities. *International Journal of Educational Management*, *19*(4), 318–329.

CHAPTER 8

DRIVING CHANGE IN HIGHER EDUCATION: STRATEGIES FOR IMPLEMENTING SUCCESSFUL ORGANIZATIONAL TRANSFORMATION

Jennifer Holland
Systemalign, USA

ABSTRACT

This chapter offers a comprehensive exploration of the complexities involved in driving organizational change within higher education institutions. Leveraging expertise in change management and industrial-organizational psychology, it provides practical insights and actionable strategies tailored for leaders spearheading transformative initiatives. Beginning with an examination of the distinct challenges and opportunities within higher education settings, the chapter delves into various frameworks and methodologies for effectively managing change. Highlighting the critical role of stakeholder engagement and fostering a culture of innovation, it outlines best practices for overcoming resistance, securing buy-in, and sustaining momentum throughout the change process. While not labeled as such, the chapter incorporates real-world examples and draws from the author's experiences to illustrate key concepts and successful implementation strategies. By offering a roadmap for navigating the intricacies of organizational change, this chapter serves as a valuable resource for leaders committed to driving meaningful transformation and fostering institutional excellence in higher education.

Keywords: Organizational change management; higher education; change initiatives; resistance; institutional effectiveness; institutional research; systems theory; systems thinking; effective change

This chapter aims to forge connections between the art and science of change management in organization development and the unique culture and needs of higher education. Utilizing insights from behavioral psychology, this exploration delves into the transformative potential of applying principles from Industrial-Organizational (IO) Psychology to navigate the dynamic landscape of academia and beyond. Change initiatives are fueled by human needs and include interventions to modify human behavior. This renders it especially susceptible to unintended negative consequences that can prove more challenging to address than the initial change intended. Cultural changes are considered large-scale interventions that even trained organizational development consultants find challenging (Anderson, 2017). Strategies to implement change successfully are included to help guide leaders and build awareness of when to include a trained professional in this area.

As an Organizational Development Consultant with over 11 years of experience in Higher Education (HE), I began my work in change management through internal roles in academia. My journey commenced with digital transformations before delving into cultural shifts. I pursued a master's in psychology, specializing in IO psychology, to apply organization development principles to my work. Deeply invested in effecting impactful changes desperately needed in higher education, I dedicated my research and thesis to change management and reducing resistance. Now certified in change delivery, I've gained invaluable insights into navigating the intricacies of organizational change within academic institutions. Initially viewing it as a temporary endeavor, I was drawn in by the numerous intelligent individuals who exhibited immense passion for their work to serve adult learners. I recognized that these people were eagerly awaiting the significant change required to drive the innovation they aspire to create and support. While I had never planned for my career to begin in higher education, I discovered that it is perhaps where my skills are most needed.

Recognizing the need to address industry-wide inconsistencies, I transitioned from internal roles to founding SystemAlign, a consulting firm dedicated to aligning people, systems, and processes across various industries. While developing SystemAlign, I continued to support higher education through my work with The Academic IO Psychologist, a consulting firm specializing in education staff coaching and leadership development. Drawing from my extensive experience in higher education and change management, I've identified four key areas for improvement: breaking down silos, fostering innovation, enhancing student support services, and aligning academia and employers' perceptions of educational value. With a background in business, psychology, and change delivery, I'm uniquely equipped to tackle these challenges. My goal for this chapter is to advance my mission of fostering growth through change.

Throughout my journey, I've gained a profound understanding of the entrenched culture within Higher Education through hands-on experience, extensive research, and industry discussions. In 2017, while collaborating with senior leaders, I was entrusted with leading several change initiatives aimed at fostering a culture rooted in assessment to enhance institutional effectiveness. These projects, aligned with the principles of Organization Development (OD), required collaborative efforts and an understanding of both internal and industry norms to navigate organizational complexities. In my exploration, I uncovered a prevalent siloed culture deeply resistant to change, significantly impacting my work in adult education.

Industrial research revealed that this pervasive culture has been operating within silos for decades (Brown, 2017; Buller, 2014; Hoopes, 2021; Hunt, 2021; Mizuta, 2022), hindering innovation and collaboration. Buller (2014) discusses cultural divisions within higher education, tracing their origins back to Snow's exploration of 'the two cultures' (Snow, 2012; as cited in Buller, 2014), which highlighted the divide between science and humanities. He further identifies a contemporary 'new divide' on the purpose of adult education, between faculty researchers, attributing holistic personal and societal development, and government officials, prioritizing job training linked to return on investment (ROI). The most recent division that I observed was between academic and administrative areas battling for power and resources. Much of the resistance to change stemmed from the need to increase resources and decision-making power in nonacademic areas. It is worth noting that neither of these divides truly considered the adult student, who requires a comprehensive approach to their education and development.

Professor Brian Rosenberg's insights in an episode of the Harvard EdCast, titled "Higher Education's Resistance to Change" (Anderson, 2023), deeply resonate with my own observations and research findings. He highlighted the pervasive resistance to change within higher education institutions, emphasizing the challenges faced by change agents. His observations led him to write a book titled "Whatever It Is, I'm Against It: Resistance to Change in Higher Education," underscoring the entrenched nature of this resistance. In my own work, I've encountered significant pushback when attempting to implement changes, often requiring extensive justification and validation of my expertise, resulting in slow progress. As Rosenberg pointed out, despite the widespread use of terms like 'transformation' and 'innovation' in college mission statements, there remains a notable disconnect and formidable resistance to change in operational practices. This resistance, deeply ingrained in the system, hinders progress, and can lead to significant setbacks.

Long-standing traditional practices and cultural norms contribute to structural inertia, fostering a culture resistant to change. Resistance to change is a reluctance to endorse revisions in workplace practices that threatens productivity, performance, and relationships (Neck et al., 2017, p. 416). It is a barrier that needs to be conquered through change management to effectively alter the behaviors of organizational members (Farkas, 2013; Battilana & Casciaro, 2013; Bradutanu, 2012). Standardization enforced through cultural fit hiring practices, and cultural behaviors ingrained in trainings, rules, policies, and procedures contribute to cultural resistance (Neck et al., 2017, p. 419). Cultural resistance, unlike regular resistance, poses a more complex challenge for change experts, requiring a comprehensive cultural shift toward change readiness and acceptance.

In my experience, change initiatives that naturally fit within the existing culture were more likely to be managed effectively and produce positive results, such as digital transformations in an online college or capacity building during growth phases. However, this was not the case with the large-scale cultural shift project previously mentioned. Despite being implemented and slowly progressing through resistance for two years, the sustainability phase brought forth covert resistance among some influential senior leaders. This resistance, characterized by public agreement while privately opposing the change and actively working against it, including instances of sabotage (Bolman & Deal, 2006, p. 449), resulted in delays, wasted resources, and high turnover among change agents, ultimately undoing much of the progress made. Reflecting on these experiences, it's clear that addressing resistance to change requires full commitment and involvement from senior leadership, including the president and change management experts. Without this support system in place, efforts to enact large-scale change are often met with obstacles and can ultimately fail to achieve their intended goals.

Despite some pioneers leading the way, most institutions have only responded to change when pressured by external forces. My early work in cultural change was driven by new requirements set forth by The Middle States Commission on Higher Education (MSCHE), a global accreditor. The amendments mandated institutions to demonstrate systematic and comprehensive approaches to assessment, pushing for transparency and accountability across all areas of operations. The 14th edition of the standards emphasized principles such as the centrality of the student experience, diversity, equity, and evidence-based decision-making (MSCHE, 14th ed., 2024). Prior to these amendments, assessment practices were confined to academic programs and student learning outcomes, leaving out critical areas of operations. This had not only resulted in a lack of data-driven decision-making across key areas critical to the success of colleges, but also hindered their ability to justify the needs for increased staffing to adequately support students.

While mandated, these imperatives were not solely driven by MSCHE; higher education faced external pressures from students and parents demanding increased transparency regarding ROI and institutional outcomes related to objectives. Reviewing these principles reveals their integral role in achieving the mission of any organization. Despite this significance, numerous colleges found themselves unprepared, resulting in discussions and articles treating organizational development concepts as new discoveries, even though these institutions are the very ones that teach these disciplines. This phenomenon was particularly striking because higher education offers an ideal environment for experiential workplace learning, recognized as a high-impact practice. Despite having direct access to the subject matter experts needed to foster innovative change, including data scientists, engineers, researchers, and other professionals, they are often excluded from relevant conversations, projects, and decisions. Even when included, their expertise may be disregarded if it goes against the grain. This failure to leverage internal resources, not only leads to missed opportunities but also contributes to resistance to change within institutions. By recognizing and addressing this issue, higher education can unlock valuable lessons to foster innovation and effectiveness.

BUILDING CHANGE READINESS: BEGIN WITH LEARNED LESSONS (THE LEARNING PHASE)

While my objective is to provide higher education leaders strategies that they can employ, it would be remiss to do so without first addressing the cultural resistance that may have hindered past attempts. These obstacles serve as valuable lessons learned, emphasizing the need to apply our collective knowledge and experiences in the field to enact the necessary solutions and changes that best serve adult learners. To effectively identify and successfully implement sustainable change within an organization or institution, it is imperative to start by reflecting on lessons learned from past experiences. This reflective process serves as the primary purpose for conducting assessments. Assessments play a crucial role in mitigating risks, avoiding the repetition of mistakes, and highlighting what is effective and worthy of replication. Through this we gain valuable insights into what has worked well, the challenges faced, and what adjustments may be necessary moving forward. Following this reflective process, conducting thorough assessments of the organization's culture, readiness, and specific needs becomes essential. In essence, starting with lessons learned sets the foundation for informed decision-making, while comprehensive assessments provide the necessary insights to develop targeted strategies for effective and sustainable change implementation.

The past few years have underscored some of the most distressing examples of the ramifications of resistance to change in higher education, with many of these effects falling on students striving to pursue their education in the aftermath of the COVID-19 pandemic. Fortunately, I worked for an online continuing education institution serving adult learners, so our program and course offerings didn't require the transition it did for others. However, we still faced challenges derived from the cultural norms of having an in-person working environment. As employers, higher education has also lagged in offering remote work opportunities, despite it being heavily supported by scientific research, dating back to Jack Nilles' pioneering telecommuting study in the 1970s. An article in Bloomberg emphasizes that Nilles recognized the necessity of a change-embracing culture for adopting innovative approaches like telecommuting, as he stated that "technology was not the limiting factor in the acceptance of telecommuting" but rather "organizational—and management—cultural changes were far more important in the rate of acceptance of telecommuting" (Gan, 2015, para. 12).

We had a readily built infrastructure in place to support the online learning environment, making the transition seamless. Unfortunately, that wasn't the case for most institutions, which had only offered a short list of courses online. This left them scrambling to integrate all in-person courses and, in some cases, entire programs into an online format. Notably, the university I worked for had opened its first online college back in 2003, nearly two decades before the COVID-19 pandemic. Additionally, online education programs had been pioneered by the University of Phoenix as far back as 1989 using CompuServe (Kentnor, 2015). These early initiatives provided ample opportunities to learn how to implement fully online programs, which have the potential to address some of the diversity, equity, inclusion, and anti-racism (DEIA) gaps that persist today. However, the slow and forced acceptance of online programs and remote work in higher education has detrimental effects on vulnerable populations. Limited offerings of online programming exclude many adult learners and first-generation students who must work, women facing childcare struggles, single parents, and others with competing demands and limited resources for whom remote options are the only feasible means for continuing their education.

People from lower socioeconomic backgrounds who are financially unable to delegate their daily responsibilities, such as grocery shopping, laundry, childcare, and other household chores often encounter significant barriers to completing degrees in tradition settings. As a young mother with a family and a full-time job, juggling multiple responsibilities, I found that enrolling in a fully online program was the only feasible way to pursue my studies and earn a graduate degree. The flexibility afforded by online education enable me to balance my various commitments and ultimately advance to the point where I can contribute insights, strategies, and solutions to the field of adult education. I recall considering a PhD program and quickly realizing that they were not designed for people with similar circumstances. While I am content with the education and credentials I have attained, I urge institutions to make PhD programs more accessible to "non-traditional" adult learners like me.

Expanding pathways and offering greater flexibility would make PhD programs more accommodating for individuals balancing work, family, and other responsibilities. For instance, providing options to earn a master's degree with the opportunity to return later to complete a PhD, rather than starting from scratch, would be immensely beneficial. Additionally, offering part-time enrollment options, even if it means a longer program duration, would enable individuals to pursue advanced degrees without compromising other aspects of their lives. Ideally, a comprehensive program would prioritize holistic development and cater to the needs of students who rely on employment to sustain themselves. Incorporating experiential learning, hands-on research, and workplace training would prepare students for real-world challenges and facilitate their transition into the workforce without the burden of having to independently market their educational value to potential employers.

Having established the case for change, step one in many change management models, I will now outline some strategies that I reference when working to foster commitment to change. In my work I combine project management, change management frameworks, organizational development, and research from various areas of psychology with a system thinking approach.

THEORIES IN PRACTICE: MOTIVATION AND COMMITMENT

Leading by example cannot be overstated in the endeavor to foster commitment within a community. As John Kotter, a prominent figure in organizational development, asserts, 'major change is impossible unless the head of the organization is an active supporter' (Kotter, 2007, p. 4). A lack of commitment from the head of the organization sends the message that the change is not a high priority and of low value with low risks of negative consequences. When individuals perceive organizational change as offering low value and carrying high risks of negative consequences, their commitment to change is likely to be compromised. There's alignment between two theories suggesting that individuals assess the costs and benefits of change initiatives based on their expectations of the outcomes and the rewards or punishments associated with them. These concepts inspire my work beginning from the top down to demonstrate commitment at the leadership level and again while planning communications with the ask to follow the lead following a bottom up approach.

I also refer to the two theories when planning my analysis for a bottom-up approach to feed information back up to leadership regarding the readiness and drivers of stakeholders' commitment to adopt change. The social exchange theory posits that an individual's commitment to change is shaped by their intentions to pursue gains while minimizing the risks of punishment (Blau, 1964, as cited in Michel et al., 2013; Gouldner, 1960, as cited in Michel et al., 2013; Cropanzano et al., 2002, as cited in Michel et al., 2013). Similarly, Vroom's expectancy theory of motivation highlights several factors influencing individuals' willingness to invest additional effort to achieve desired outcomes, such as expectancy, self-efficacy, perceived value, and anticipated rewards or consequences (Vroom, 1964, as cited in Cooper et al., 2017). Based on these theories, I structure some of my semi-structured interview and survey questions around these factors. As one might infer, if this occurs after employing the concepts in the top-down step, an intervention is already in place, potentially altering their measures of readiness.

Organizational leaders must carefully consider these factors when implementing change strategies, ensuring that the perceived benefits outweigh the perceived costs to motivate employees to embrace and actively participate in the change process. To achieve this, leaders must first understand the perceived losses through an openness to listening, with the intent of applying what is learned to the change initiative. Failure to adopt this mindset and practice is likely to result in a loss of trust. Therefore, it is advisable to refrain from asking questions without the intent of following up with actions that align with the responses. Trust is a critical component of change management, as recognized in many frameworks. Active listening, including stakeholders at all levels, can help identify a coalition of change leaders, mitigate resistance, empower others, raise awareness of the problem, build commitment and ability, work toward a shared vision, and harness collective knowledge to begin planning as a community of change-makers.

Many of the opportunities to build commitment and begin to foster the adoption of the change present themselves through the active listening and communication steps within change management. I use these opportunities to employ as much scientific research as possible customizing it as I go, to meet the needs that I hear from stakeholders. The involvement of top leadership is essential not only to maintain their own commitment but also to gain additional insights into the college's operational dynamics within its mission and to adopt a systems thinking approach to change. It is through these phases that I learn about the interconnectivity of cross-functions within an organization and identify the disconnects and opportunities to build alignment.

APPLYING SYSTEMS THINKING FOR STRATEGIC ALIGNMENT

Systems theory provides a foundation for understanding and addressing complexity in organizational systems (Adams et al., 2013). Building on this foundation, systems thinking was introduced by Richmond in 1994 and emphasizes holistic analysis, dynamic assessment, and goal-oriented decision-making (Arnold & Wade, 2015). I always push for viewing the institution through the lens of the relationships, interconnections, and its interdependent components, as alignment is not possible without doing so. Failure to have a holistic understanding of the institution leads to disconnects between interdependent units and between the head of the organization and the stakeholders in the organization. When taking a systems thinking approach, you evaluate patterns and ways that they interact to inform proactive decision-making (Buckle Henning et al., 2012). Meadows (2008) identified three components of systems thinking relevant to understanding the whole organization. The components include elements (characteristics of the organization), interconnections (relationships between the elements of the organization), and purpose (mission, goals, and/or function). An illustrative example is provided below (see Figure 1) to demonstrate how strategic goal alignment connects assessment (elements) to the institutional mission (purpose) through cross-departmental interconnections.

I've applied this framework in adult education to enhance stakeholder engagement and foster cross-collaborations by facilitating the understanding of individuals' and departmental roles and functions within the institution. In assessment workshops, I've challenged members from various departments to align their goals to both the mission statement and strategic plan objectives. This exercise encourages stakeholders at all levels, from leadership to staff, to recognize the interconnections among the functions within the college system, thereby promoting alignment. This approach not only cultivates cohesion but also provides opportunities for cross-collaboration rather than operating in silos. Through this process, I've observed that many stakeholders were surprised to discover overlapping goals across departments in their assessment planning, despite each unit having distinct measures. They've also learned to incorporate collective and individual

Figure 1 Utilizing a system thinking approach to metric building to break silos in academia (Holland & Danz-Lopez, 2023), presented at The Academic IO Summit.

lessons into their outcomes and strategies for closing the assessment loop. Such efforts result in greater alignment and stakeholder engagement, fostering autonomy and empowering stakeholders to embrace innovative approaches to cross-functional collaborations. As stakeholder engagement grows, individuals collaborate to develop a shared vision, a crucial aspect of effective change management.

I urge leadership to embrace this critical transformation, laying the foundation for agility and readiness to drive innovative change and ensure the sustainability of growth. Change is inevitable; it can either continue to happen passively or be proactively created. In the realm of adult education, where diverse learners with varied backgrounds and needs are served, embracing this transformational mindset is crucial for creating inclusive learning environments that foster lifelong learning and personal development. Adopting a change readiness and holistic approach to adult education is increasingly crucial in the wake of rapid advancements in AI and the digital landscape. The world is in a constant state of innovation, and the adult learning environment must contribute to this by helping its graduates build competitive advantages and the ability to articulate their program learning outcomes to the real world. It is essential to view the organization as a cohesive system, while working toward common goals derived from a shared vision rooted in the overarching mission and values. All initiatives should align with the organization's mission and vision, fostering cross-functionality among departments and teams. Moreover, they should incorporate measures that can be assessed and reported by multiple units, demonstrating how the institution fulfills its mission and objectives. While challenging, this approach cannot thrive in a siloed culture and is indispensable for alignment, continuous learning, and ongoing improvement—all critical components of institutional effectiveness. Achieving institutional effectiveness means being in a position where external changes allow you to highlight your contributions to it, rather than merely reacting to it.

REFERENCES

Adams, K. M., Hester, P. T., Bradley, J. M., Meyers, T. J., & Keating, C. B. (2013). Systems theory as the foundation for understanding systems. *Systems Engineering*, *17*(1), 112–123. https://doi.org/10.1002/sys.21255

Anderson, D. L. (2017). *Organizational development: The process of leading organizational change* (4th ed.). SAGE Publications.

Anderson, J. (2023). *Higher education's resistance to change*. Harvard Graduate School of Education. https://www.gse.harvard.edu/ideas/edcast/23/11/higher-educations-resistasnce-change

Arnold, R. D., & Wade, J. P. (2015). A definition of systems thinking: A systems approach. *Procedia Computer Science*, *44*, 669–678. https://doi.org/10.1016/j.procs.2015.03.050

Battilana, J. & Casciaro, T. (2013). Overcoming resistance to organizational change: Strong ties and affective cooptation. *Management Science*, *59*(4), 819-836. https://doi.org/10.1287/mnsc.1120.1583

Bolman, L. G., & Deal, T. E. (2006). Reframing change. In J. V. Gallos (Ed.), *Organizational development: A Jossey-Bass reader* (pp. 447–469). Jossey-Bass.

Bradutanu, D. (2012). Identifying the reducing resistance to change phase in an organizational change model. *Acta Universitatis Danubius: Oeconomica*, *8*(2), 18–26.

Brown, J. T. (2017). The seven silos of accountability in higher education: Systematizing multiple logics and fields. *Research & Practice in Assessment*, *11*, 41–58.

Buckle Henning, P., Wilmhurst, J., & Yearworth, M. (2012). Understanding systems thinking: An agenda for applied research in industry. In *Proceedings of the 56th annual meeting of the ISSS - 2012*. https://journals.isss.org/index.php/proceedings56th/article/view/1909

Buller, J. L. (2014). The two cultures of higher education in the twenty-first century and their impact on academic freedom. *AAUP*, (5). https://www.aaup.org/JAF5/two-cultures-higher-education-twenty-first-century-and-their-impact-academic-freedom

Cooper, K., Ashley, M., & Brownell, S. (2017). Using expectancy value theory as a framework to reduce student resistance to active learning: A proof of concept. *Journal of Microbiology & Biology Education*, *18*(2), 1–8. https://doi.org/10.1128/jmbe.v18i2.1289

Farkas, M. G. (2013). Building and sustaining a culture of assessment: Best practices for change leadership. *Reference Services Review*, *41*(1), 13–31. https://doi.org/10.1108/00907321311300857

Gan, V. (2015, December 1). *What telecommuting looked like in 1973*. Bloomberg. https://www.bloomberg.com/news/articles/2015-12-01/what-telecommuting-looked-like-in-1973?embedded-checkout=true

Holland, J., & Danz-Lopez, S. D. (2023). *Utilizing a systems thinking approach to metric building to break silos in academia* [Conference presentation]. The Academic IO 2023, Virtual Summit.

Hoopes, L. (2021, September 9). *Silos are everywhere in higher education*. RNL Education Insights Blog. https://www.ruffalonl.com/blog/enrollment/silos-are-everywhere-in-higher-education/

Hunt, J. (2021, March 17). *Death to silos*. Inside Higher Ed. https://www.insidehighered.com/blogs/call-action-marketing-and-communications-higher-education/death-silos

Kentnor, H. (2015). Distance education and the evolution of online learning in the United States. *Curriculum and Teaching Dialogue, 17*(1 & 2). University of Denver Sturm College of Law Digital Commons @ DU website: https://digitalcommons.du.edu/cgi/viewcontent.cgi?article=1026&context=law_facpub

Kotter, J. P. (2007). Leading change: Why transformation efforts fail. *Harvard Business Review, 85*(1), 4–12.

Meadows, D. H. (2008). *Thinking in systems: A primer*. Chelsea Green Publishing.

Michel, A., Todnem, R., & Burnes, B. (2013). The limitations of diagnosis and the need for a return to organisational change: Re-thinking change agency in the 21st century. *Journal of Organizational Change Management, 26*(2), 217–234. https://doi.org/10.1108/09534811311328416

Mizuta, M. S. (2022). *Silos in higher education institutions: Shifting from organizational phenomena to a practical framework for equitable decision-making*. Dissertations and Theses. Paper 6105 (https://doi.org/10.15760/etd.7965

Neck, C. P., Houghton, J. D., & Murray, E. J. (2017). *Organizational behavior: A critical thinking approach*. Sage publication.

Snow, C. P. (2012). *The two cultures: And a second look—An expanded version of "the two cultures and the scientific revolution"*. Cambridge University Press.

CHAPTER 9

ANDRAGOGY IN ONLINE EDUCATION: EMPOWERING ADULT LEARNERS

Marcedes Butler
UNLV College of Education, USA

ABSTRACT

Rooted in andragogy (Knowles, 1973, 1980, 1984, 1988), this chapter serves as a practical guide for online faculty members, exploring its real-world applications in adult education. Drawing from the autoethnography of a faculty administrator's educational and professional experiences, it offers tangible strategies for empowering fully online adult learners. By spotlighting the six andragogy principles—self-concept, learner experience, readiness to learn, orientation, motivation, and active learning, it provides real-world insights into integrating diversity, equity, inclusion, and anti-racism (DEIA) principles into online teaching practices.

Keywords: Andragogy; adult education; online education; workforce development; DEIA

INTRODUCTION

As a scholar-practitioner deeply immersed in adult education, my goal in this book chapter is to explore how faculty can apply Malcolm Knowles's six principles of andragogy and adapt them to incorporate diversity, equity, inclusion, and anti-racism (DEIA) focused learning activities for online adult learners. Andragogy, the art of teaching adults, contrasts with pedagogy, the traditional approach to teaching children (Forrest & Peterson, 2006; Loeng, 2017). The core principle of andragogy is that adults, being more motivated and self-aware than children, require learning experiences centered around their lived experiences rather than solely academic content (Knowles, 1980; Merriam et al., 2020). The six principles of andragogy, including experience, self-concept, readiness to learn, problem-centered learning, and motivation, are the foundation for designing effective adult learning experiences (Knowles, 1973, 1980, 1984, 1988). These principles help faculty adopt teaching methods and practices that forge meaningful connections with adult students, ensuring that diverse learner needs are met and valued (Garrison, 2016; Merriam & Bierema, 2013). Understanding and applying the principles of andragogy were crucial to my success as a working adult student and significantly enhanced my effectiveness as an administrator and faculty member advising nontraditional, working adult undergraduate and graduate students.

This chapter provides a comprehensive guide on adult education strategies grounded in theory and enriched by practice (Tough, 1971; Brookfield, 2015; Knowles, 1988). It is designed for faculty aiming to create engaging, equitable, and inclusive online learning environments for adult learners. Drawing on my experience as an administrator, faculty member, and online student, I offer practical strategies to integrate these principles into online courses. My dual roles have deepened my understanding of adult learners' challenges and needs, enhancing my ability to support and guide them effectively. In the following chapters, I will share my narrative, addressing themes of diversity, equity, and inclusion, and detailing the strategies in my efforts to foster success in online adult education, all through the lens of andragogical principles. This exploration aims to offer valuable insights and practical approaches to enhance the online learning experience for both faculty members and learners.

MY PATH IN ONLINE ADULT EDUCATION

Embarking on an autoethnographic journey within adult education, I am Dr. Marcedes Butler, a Research Associate in the College of Education at the University of Nevada, Las Vegas (UNLV), and a Boys & Girls Club of

Southern Nevada (BGCSNV) Fellow. With nearly two decades of experience as both a full-time student and staff member, my professional background spans academic advisement, research, administrative, and faculty roles that promote student success and persistence to graduation for all students. My TEDxUNLV talk, "Degree Completion: How Finishing College Changes Lives," emphasizes the transformative impact of degree attainment and highlights the importance of creating pathways that support students' persistence (TEDx, 2024). Additionally, I have been a fully online student during the COVID-19 pandemic. These diverse experiences have profoundly shaped my approach to adult education, particularly in integrating DEIA principles.

My educational background includes a Doctorate in Educational Psychology from the University of Southern California (USC) and a Master of Science in Counseling in Student Development in Higher Education from California State University, Long Beach (CSULB). I completed the online Equity Institute course at UNLV, which advances faculty and staff understanding of core DEIA issues and addresses biases that could hinder student achievement (University of Nevada, Las Vegas, 2021). Additionally, I participated in CornellX's TLDC101x: Teaching & Learning in the Diverse Classroom, which explored strategies for inclusive course design and student-centered pedagogical practices (Equity Institute Helps Address Practices That May Hamper Student Success, 2024). During the pandemic in 2021, I also earned a Graduate Certificate in Nonprofit Management at UNLV. These experiences have provided me with practical insights into applying theory to practice and utilizing adult learning theoretical frameworks like andragogy, proposed by Malcolm Knowles (1973), to guide my approach. By aligning DEIA principles with andragogical practices, I aim to foster inclusive and empowering online learning environments.

Professionally, my involvement with the MGM College Opportunity Program (COP) has been pivotal. This innovative workforce development degree completion program, the first-ever partnership between a statewide higher education system and a Fortune 500 company, provided comprehensive online educational opportunities for MGM employees through tuition assistance (Butler, 2023; MGM Resorts International Employees—NSHE, 2023). As the College Opportunity Learning Concierge, I served as a dedicated liaison for program participants, collaborating with various university departments to create proactive, intrusive, and wraparound support services. These efforts enhanced persistence and retention, addressed academic issues, and reduced administrative barriers. As a faculty member at UNLV, I teach Research Methods, First-Year Seminar, Second-Year Seminar, and elective courses to working adults enrolled in the Nevada Forward™ Undergraduate Apprenticeship Program (UAP). These courses are delivered in asynchronous learning environments, which offer flexibility but require students to be self-disciplined and focused (Purwati et al., 2022). Effective instruction in these settings necessitates a well-designed learning path (Zhou et al., 2023). My experience as a full-time online student informs my approach to creating interactive learning environments, and as the founder of AcademicHelp101.com, I provide educational consulting that helps institutions and students enhance their educational processes and improve degree completion rates.

My work and research are deeply intertwined with DEIA principles. Navigating the intersection of gender, ethnicity, and other identities presents both challenges and opportunities in adult education. As a Black woman administrator and faculty member, I have encountered stereotypes and biases that can undermine my authority and expertise (Butler, 2023; Butler & Whitehead, 2022). These challenges have driven me to advocate for greater academic representation and diversity. By openly embracing my identity and experiences, I strive to create an inclusive environment that supports all learners. Through teaching, advocacy, and research, I aim to dismantle barriers and create equitable pathways to education.

THEORETICAL FRAMEWORK: SIX PRINCIPLES OF ANDRAGOGY

Andragogy, which originated in the 19th century with Alexander Kapp and was later popularized by Knowles (1973, 1980, 1984, 1988), forms the foundation for understanding adult learning and guiding teaching methodologies (Knowles et al., 2014; Loeng, 2017). Knowles' seminal work, especially his 1973 book "The Adult Learner," has been pivotal in shaping modern perspectives on adult education. The core of andragogy consists of six key assumptions or principles that guide the design and implementation of adult learning experiences. Initially, Knowles (1980) presented four assumptions: building on adults' prior experiences, recognizing their readiness to learn, acknowledging their need to know, and focusing on problem-centered learning. As the field evolved, Knowles introduced two additional assumptions in 1984: the intrinsic motivation of adult learners and their responsibility for learning. This expansion led to a framework encompassing six principles, reflecting a deeper understanding of adult learning processes.

These principles guide faculty in designing and implementing instructional strategies tailored to the unique characteristics and needs of adult learners. By incorporating DEIA principles into andragogical strategies, faculty can create collaborative online learning environments that empower adult learners and enhance their success. As adult education evolves, andragogy serves as a crucial framework for faculty aiming to address the diverse needs of adult learners in the 21st century and beyond.

In summary, andragogical principles have been essential in developing strategies that empower online adult learners, foster intrinsic motivation, and ensure practical applications of knowledge (Knowles, 1973, 1980, 1984, 1988). By focusing on adults' prior experiences, problem-centered learning, and self-directed education, I have created relevant and responsive coursework. My approach, which incorporates digital tools and personalized support, aligns with andragogical principles and enhances the learning experience for diverse adult learners. I have seen firsthand how these principles create a more inclusive and effective educational experience. They have guided me in developing strategies that reflect the diverse backgrounds and learning preferences of online adult students, resulting in improved outcomes and greater satisfaction. As adult education advances, andragogy remains a vital framework for adapting teaching practices to meet the complex and diverse needs of online adult learners (Zhou et al., 2023).

PRINCIPLES OF ANDRAGOGY & DEIA IN ADULT LEARNING ENVIRONMENTS

Understanding adult learners' unique characteristics and needs is crucial for crafting effective teaching and learning experiences. Cultivating DEIA in online adult learning environments is essential for fostering equitable access and promoting meaningful engagement among all learners (Tomlin & Cupid, 2023). The six foundational assumptions that reinforce the design of adult learning experiences offer valuable insights into adult learners' motivations, preferences, and behaviors, informing Facultys' approaches to curriculum development, pedagogy, and classroom practices (Knowles et al., 2014).

This section explores Knowles' six principles of andragogy and provides strategies for integrating them into DEIA-focused online teaching practices for adult learners:

1. Need to Know

    Adults must understand the relevance and purpose behind their learning (Knowles, 1980, 1984, 2014). Knowing why they need to learn something fosters motivation and engagement in the learning process (Knowles, 2014; Tough, 1979). When adults perceive the personal benefits or consequences of learning, they are more likely to actively participate and invest energy in the educational experience (Knowles, 1984; Merriam & Bierema, 2013). Communicating the objectives and benefits of learning the content can help learners understand its relevance and foster a deeper understanding and commitment to learning objectives (Kosslyn, 2021). By incorporating DEIA principles into active learning strategies, faculty can create online courses that foster a culture of inclusivity, respect, and empowerment where every learner feels valued and supported (Brookfield, 2015; Tomlin & Cupid, 2023).

Learning Activities:
- **Personal Anecdotes:** Invite students to share personal anecdotes or examples related to the course material through discussion forums or multimedia presentations.
- **Diverse Perspectives:** Integrate diverse perspectives and voices into course materials, such as readings or guest speakers, to provide a range of viewpoints and experiences.
- **Design Collaborative Projects:** Create group projects or collaborative assignments that allow students to learn from each other's experiences and perspectives, promoting peer-to-peer learning and knowledge exchange.

Personal Experience: In my practice, I have made it a priority to clearly communicate the relevance of course materials by linking them directly to real-world applications. For example, in a research course, I invited students to share their personal work experiences and discussed how course concepts could address real challenges they face. This approach not only highlighted the importance of the material but also fostered a more inclusive and engaged learning environment.

2. The Role of the Learners' Experiences

Knowles emphasized the significance of tapping into learners' diverse life experiences to enrich learning (Brookfield, 2015; Knowles, 1984). This assumption highlights the value of integrating activities that resonate with students' prior knowledge and backgrounds. It is crucial to create opportunities for learners to share their personal experiences and expertise through group projects, interactive discussions, and reflective activities, as this fosters deeper engagement, enhances collaborative learning, and promotes critical reflection (Conaway & Zorn-Arnold, 2015; Forrest & Peterson, 2006). Faculty can enhance relatability by incorporating activities such as case studies, role-plays, and journals that incorporate DEIA concepts (Brookfield, 2015; Kosslyn, 2021).

Learning Activities:
- **Personal Experience Sharing:** Facilitate group discussions where students share personal anecdotes or experiences relevant to course topics, promoting peer-to-peer learning and understanding.

- **Evolution of Course Content:** Encourage students to suggest additional readings or case studies based on their diverse backgrounds and experiences.
- **Broadening Exposure and Understanding:** Infuse course materials with various viewpoints and voices, including readings or guest speakers from diverse backgrounds.

    Personal Experience: I have found that encouraging students to share their diverse experiences in discussion forums has significantly enriched the learning environment. For instance, when discussing case studies, students often draw on their unique professional backgrounds, which helps everyone gain a broader perspective and deepens the understanding of course concepts.

3. The Learners' Self-Concept

    Self-directedness epitomizes adult learners' ability to make independent choices and decisions and assume responsibility for their outcomes (Conaway & Zorn-Arnold, 2015; Knowles, 1980, 2014). Adult learners naturally gravitate toward autonomy and are strongly inclined toward self-direction (Deci & Ryan, 2012; Knowles, 1984). Faculty are pivotal in embracing self-directed learning, offering diverse resources and learning pathways to personalize the educational experience (Garrison, 2016; Kosslyn, 2021). In online teaching, faculty empower learners to establish their learning goals within course objectives, fostering opportunities for cocreating learning goals, selecting projects, and engaging in decision-making processes (Brookfield, 2015; Forrest & Peterson, 2006). Faculty can enhance their DEIA principles by fostering a supportive, inclusive learning environment that honors each learner's diverse backgrounds and perspectives (Kosslyn, 2021).

    Learning Activities:
    - **Student-Led Initiatives:** Integrate opportunities for students to lead discussions or initiatives promoting diversity, equity, and inclusion within the online learning community.
    - **Learning Goal Collaboration:** Encourage students to collaborate in defining learning objectives for the course or specific units, allowing them to take ownership of their learning trajectory.
    - **Choice-Based Projects:** Offer a variety of project options related to course content, enabling students to select projects aligned with their interests and learning styles.

        Personal Experience: I have actively involved students in setting their own learning goals and project choices, which has led to increased engagement and ownership of their learning process. For example, allowing students to select project topics based on their interests has resulted in more meaningful and personalized learning experiences that reflect their individual perspectives and backgrounds.

4. Readiness to Learn

According to Knowles (1984), adults become ready to learn when they perceive the knowledge or skills taught as relevant to their social and professional environments. This highlights the importance of aligning course content with students' challenges, goals, and everyday experiences (Knowles, 2014). Faculty play a crucial role in promoting learning readiness in online classrooms by assisting learners in identifying their learning needs and goals and providing personalized support and resources (Purwati et al., 2022). Moreover, providing students with opportunities to explore topics of personal or professional interest within the course curriculum can further boost their motivation and engagement (Conaway & Zorn-Arnold, 2015; Kosslyn, 2021). By creating a DEIA learning environment, faculty can help students overcome barriers to learning and enhance their readiness to tackle new challenges (Garrison, 2016).

Learning Activities:
- **Collaborative Goal Setting:** Facilitate group activities where learners with similar learning objectives collaborate to set common goals and support each other throughout the course.
- **Personalized Learning Support:** Offer personalized learning pathways or resources based on students' readiness levels and preferences.
- **Collaborative Engagement:** Encourage collaborative discussions and projects that foster community and shared learning experiences among students.

Personal Experience: In my practice, I have tailored course content to address the specific challenges and goals of my students, which has greatly improved their readiness and enthusiasm for learning. For example, integrating current issues related to students' professional fields into the coursework has helped them see the immediate relevance of their studies and stay engaged.

5. Problem-Centered Learning

Adult learners are motivated to learn when they perceive its relevance to solving real-life problems or achieving specific tasks (Deci & Ryan, 2012; Knowles, 1984). This assumption highlights the importance of designing learning activities that resonate with learners' practical needs and experiences. Faculty should emphasize process-based learning by allowing students to apply their knowledge to practical scenarios or case studies (Forrest & Peterson, 2006; Merriam & Bierema, 2013). Encouraging students to explore how course learning outcomes can be used in real-life situations further reinforces the material's relevance and importance (Kosslyn, 2021; Purwati et al., 2022). Faculty can ensure that course content reflects the principles of DEIA by empowering adult learners to apply their knowledge and skills, fostering an appreciation for diverse perspectives (Conaway & Zorn-Arnold, 2015; Garrison, 2016).

Learning Activities:
- **Real-World Problem Solving:** Assign tasks or projects that require learners to apply course concepts to real-world problems or scenarios.
- **Case Studies:** Use case studies or simulations that reflect practical challenges in students' professional fields, promoting problem-solving and critical thinking.
- **Community-Based Projects:** Engage learners in community-based projects that address local or global issues, encouraging practical application of their knowledge.

Personal Experience: I have incorporated real-world case studies and problem-solving activities into my courses to enhance their relevance and application. For example, students work on projects that address contemporary issues in their fields, which has significantly increased their motivation and engagement.

6. Motivation to Learn

Adults are predominantly motivated by internal factors, such as personal growth and fulfillment, rather than external rewards (Deci & Ryan, 2012; Merriam & Bierema, 2013). Understanding the intrinsic motivations that drive adult learners can help faculty design more effective learning experiences (Knowles, 2014; Tough, 1979). To cultivate motivation, faculty should provide opportunities for learners to pursue their interests and set personal goals within the course framework (Conaway & Zorn-Arnold, 2015; Kosslyn, 2021). By recognizing and validating learners' intrinsic motivations and providing supportive, inclusive environments, educators can enhance learners' engagement and persistence (Garrison, 2016; Conaway & Zorn-Arnold, 2015).

Learning Activities:
- **Goal Setting:** Encourage learners to set personal learning goals and align course objectives with their intrinsic motivations.
- **Choice and Autonomy:** Provide opportunities for students to choose topics or projects that resonate with their interests and aspirations.

- **Recognition and Feedback:** Offer constructive feedback and recognize learners' achievements to validate their progress and intrinsic motivation.

  Personal Experience: I have observed that when students are given the autonomy to choose projects that align with their personal interests and career goals, their motivation and engagement levels increase. For instance, allowing students to pursue topics they are passionate about has led to more meaningful and sustained learning experiences.

CONCLUSION

In conclusion, fostering DEIA in online adult learning environments is crucial for creating genuinely inclusive educational experiences (Tomlin & Cupid, 2023; Kosslyn, 2021; Purwati et al., 2022; Knowles). Integrating Malcolm Knowles' six assumptions of andragogy with equity-minded and anti-racist principles equips faculty to effectively address the diverse needs of adult learners and promote equitable outcomes. This approach emphasizes the importance of active engagement and the practical application of knowledge in fostering a supportive learning environment. This integration ensures that all learners, regardless of their background, feel valued and supported. It enhances the educational experience by creating an environment where diverse perspectives are acknowledged and respected (Loeng, 2017).

Recognizing that adult learners are active participants in their education, rather than passive recipients of information, is essential (Knowles, 1973, 1980, 1984, 1988). This understanding empowers learners to take ownership of their educational journey, leading to deeper engagement and improved learning outcomes. By aligning online instructional strategies with adult learners' characteristics and needs, faculty can enhance student success (Kosslyn, 2021). Active learning techniques, such as group discussions, case studies, debates, and role-playing, facilitate the analysis, synthesis, and evaluation of concepts while encouraging reflection on personal attitudes and values (Conaway & Zorn-Arnold, 2015; Knowles et al., 2014; Kosslyn, 2021; Purwati et al., 2022). These methods ensure that learning is not only relevant but also applicable to real-world contexts.

Moving forward, the insights shared in this chapter serve as a call to action for faculty members to embrace their roles in online adult education with renewed vigor and purpose. By adhering to these principles, faculty can drive meaningful change and create environments where all adult learners can thrive. This commitment to inclusivity and effective teaching strategies not only improves educational outcomes but also contributes to a more equitable and supportive educational landscape (Knowles et al., 2014).

REFERENCES

Brookfield, S. D. (2015). *The skillful teacher: On technique, trust, and responsiveness in the classroom.* John Wiley & Sons.
Butler, M. (2023). DO NOT CALL ME MISS. *Still Working While Black: The Untold Stories of Student Affairs Practitioners (25).*
Butler, M., & Whitehead, M. (2022). Did you get the memo?: Black leadership and the climb. In *African American leadership and mentoring through purpose, preparation, and preceptors* (pp. 101–125). IGI Global.
Conaway, W., & Zorn-Arnold, B. (2015). The keys to online learning for adults. *Distance Learning, 12*(4), 37–42.
Deci, E. L., & Ryan, R. M. (2012). Self-determination theory. *Handbook of theories of social psychology, 1*(20), 416–436.
Equity institute helps address practices that May hamper student success. (2024, May 3).University of Nevada, Las Vegas. https://www.unlv.edu/news/article/equity-institute-helps-address-practices-may-hamper-student-success
Forrest III, S. P., & Peterson, T. O. (2006). It's called andragogy. *Academy of management learning & education, 5*(1), 113–122.
Garrison, D. R. (2016). *E-learning in the 21st century: A community of inquiry framework for research and practice.* Routledge.
Knowles, M. (1973). *The adult learner: A neglected species.* Gulf.
Knowles, M. (1980, August). *My farewell address: Andragogy—No panacea, No ideology.* Training and Development Journal .
Knowles, M. (1984). *Andragogy in action.* Jossey-Bass.
Knowles, M. (1988). *The adult learner: A neglected species* (3rd ed.). Gulf.
Knowles, M. S., Holton, E. F., & Swanson, R. A. (2014). *The adult learner: The definitive classic in adult education and human resource development* (8th ed.). Routledge.
Kosslyn, S. M. (2021). *Visual learning and memory: Techniques for effective teaching.* Cambridge University Press.
Loeng, S. (2017). Alexander Kapp–the first known user of the andragogy concept. *International Journal of Lifelong Education, 36*(6), 629–643.
Merriam, S. B., & Baumgartner, L. M. (2020). *Learning in adulthood: A comprehensive guide.* John Wiley & Sons.
Merriam, S. B., & Bierema, L. L. (2013). *Adult learning: Linking theory and practice.* John Wiley & Sons.
MGM resorts international employees – NSHE. (2023). Nevada.edu. https://nshe.nevada.edu/mgm-employees/
Purwati, D., Mardhiah, A., Nurhasanah, E., & Ramli, R. (2022). The six characteristics of andragogy and future research directions in EFL: A literature review. *Elsya: Journal of English Language Studies, 4*(1), 86–95.
TEDx. (2024, June 11). *How finishing college changes your life | Dr Marcedes Butler | TEDxUNLV.* YouTube. [Video]. https://youtu.be/U1F3rNov5J8?si=9mWWT8B-74cWzhTT

Tomlin, A. D. & Cupid, S. (Eds.) (2023), *Voices of the field: DEIA champions in higher education*. IAP.

Tough, A. (1971). *The adult's learning projects. A fresh approach to theory and practice in adult learning.*

Tough, A. M (1979). *The adult's learning projects: A fresh approach to theory and practice in adult learning (No. 1)*. Ontario Institute for Studies in Education.

Zhou, X., Smith, C. J. M., & Al-Samarraie, H. (2023). Digital technology adaptation and initiatives: A systematic review of teaching and learning during COVID-19. *Journal of computing in higher education*, 1–22.

ADDITIONAL RESOURCES

Teaching & learning in the diverse classroom online course | Center for Teaching Innovation. (n.d.). https://teaching.cornell.edu/programs/faculty-instructors/faculty-institutes/teaching-learning-diverse-classroom-online-course

CHAPTER 10

PROMOTING FLEXIBILITY AS A MEANS OF SUCCESS FOR ADULT LEARNERS

Joyvina Evans
Howard University, USA

ABSTRACT

Adult learners, often; called nontraditional learners, are typically 25 years or olderand come from diverse backgrounds. They face unique challenges that can delay their studies, including full-time employment and family responsibilities. Motivation to earn a degree varies, but research shows higher graduation rates when the degree supports career advancement (Bellare et al., 2023). Common barriers include balancing work and life, reducing work hours to fit course schedules, and completing coursework on time. This chapter highlights the importance of fostering inclusion and belonging for adult learners through flexible learning options, scheduling, and assignment deadlines. Online learning appeals to many adults due to its flexibility and the elimination of commuting. However, some online programs include synchronous components, like live sessions, which may pose scheduling challenges. To support success, courses should be fully asynchronous or offer live sessions at convenient times—such as lunchtime, early mornings, or weekdays—with recorded options available. Effective faculty-student engagement that recognizes the complex needs of adult learners is essential. This approach balances accountability with empathy, helping adult learners manage their commitments while progressing toward their educational goals.

Keywords: Adult learners; non-traditional students; flexible learning; online; education; work-life balance

INTRODUCTION

Adult learners, also known as nontraditional learners, are diverse and generally a minimum of 25 years of age (Penn State, 2016). With age comes additional responsibilities and challenges. Many adult learners have challenges that may delay their course of study and tend to have a schedule that includes full-time employment and family responsibilities. Like all learners, the motivation to earn an undergraduate or graduate degree can vary based on life circumstances and their own personal and professional goals. Their motivation for a degree varies. According to Bellare et al. (2023), there is an increased graduation rate when the degree is connected to work advancement. Research shows that balancing work-life, decreasing work hours to accommodate course schedules, and completing coursework are barriers to success. This chapter will share the need for the inclusion and belonging of adult learners through flexible learning options, flexible scheduling, and flexible assignment due dates.

HOW WORK RELATES TO DEIA

Diversity, equity, inclusion, and accessibility are at the forefront of my approaches to supporting adult learners. Understanding that all adults have different circumstances, experiences, life lessons, finances, and responsibilities is essential for the success of adult learners. Many adult learners feel they do not have time to further their education, therefore having flexibility eases the burden and alleviates some of the time and stress barriers As such, flexibility in adult education is vital. It is estimated that approximately 16–19% of college learners need appropriate technology, and of those learners, approximately 20–30% are classified as having lower incomes. This lack of technology also means that roughly 27% of US adults need appropriate internet at home, which may pose difficulties completing coursework (MHEC, 2021).

These statistics lend to the fact that there are learners who have an unfair advantage and do not have the appropriate resources. If learners are at traditional brick-and-mortar campuses, they may be able to use the libraries at their college or university. However, if they are nontraditional students, they may need to find resources, books, and support online or at public libraries Additionally, while we are in a technological society, it is important to note that everyone does not have a computer, laptop, or iPad at home.

Even with the inclusion of computers in public libraries, sometimes the libraries may be inaccessible, or they have hours of operation that could be more conducive to the learner's work or family obligations.

THEORETICAL/CONCEPTUAL FRAMEWORK

Andragogy is a term that has been used for centuries and has many reiterations. Malcolm Knowles popularized the "andragogy" theory because he constantly used the term as a synonym for adult learning and adult education, which describes the science behind how adults learn. Andragogy and Pedagogy are distinct in that there are differences in how adults learn vs children. Andragogy is a learning-center approach that describes adults as self-directed, whereas pedagogy involves a teacher-centered approach (Niksadat et al., 2022). Andragogy has six principles or assumptions, including the need to know, self-concept, experience, readiness, orientation, and motivation.

The second assumption of self-concept is the central assumption that tends to guide adult learning. Self-concept focuses on how many adults prefer lives and learning that are autonomous and self-directed. As someone who completed traditional and nontraditional education programs, the autonomy and flexibility was vital. I worked full-time and needed flexibility due to other professional and personal obligations. I was already working in at a hospital, so I was able to share some of my experiences in the online discussion boards. Adult learners are independent and like to make decisions and manage their time, lives, and learning. This leads to the importance of flexible educational opportunities for adult learners. They can direct their schedule and knowledge. Adult learning makes students use their work, life experiences, and self-reflection to take responsibility for their education and overall learning (Brown, E.A., Kinder, H., Stang, G., & Shumbert, W., 2023).

CHALLENGES

Time management is one of the top challenges in adult learning. As discussed, adults are trying to juggle and balance many commitments. Adult learners tend to have more commitments due to work, commuting, family, and personal responsibilities. The restrictions associated with traditional classrooms and learning can cause stress and harm and may hinder their desire to advance their education. There is an opportunity to provide time management courses and assistance with scheduling to help with obligations.

The flexibility involved with adult learners can lead to challenges for faculty. For instance, if there are no due dates or penalties for late submissions, faculty can find themselves grading almost daily. This can pose challenges to work-life balance and cause burnout for faculty. Ensuring that leadership is lenient with faculty grading deadlines helps mitigate this challenge.

While these are only a few of the myriad of challenges, it is still important to note that the strengths and benefits far outweigh the challenges and weaknesses. Providing an opportunity for adults to further their education is beneficial to them, their well-being and overall equity, but also society as a whole.

RECOMMENDATIONS

While there are a myriad of challenges, it is important to note that there are even more opportunities. The attraction to online learning is due to the flexibility and the removal of having to drive to campus. It is important to note that some online programs have synchronous components, such as live session days and times, that can lead to challenges. A few recommendations for student success are:

1. For success, 100% asynchronous courses or live session days and times that accommodate adult learners are needed. The accommodation could include sessions during lunchtime, weekdays, early morning sessions (before work) or later night sessions, and allowing students to listen to recordings with a brief knowledge check or reflection to attest their understanding of the live content.
2. Ensuring that live content or live lectures are not passive but contain some form of engagement, clear objectives, relevant topics, and connect to adult learners' real-life experiences are areas that must be considered.
3. Record lectures so that adult learners who cannot attend due to an emergency or other obligations can still hear the lecture and stay engaged with the faculty and classmates. Additionally, when delivering the lecture, the classroom must have different communication and learning styles and types. Therefore, faculty should consider the delivery as well as the visual components (video, slides, discussion, etc).
4. Flexibility includes due dates of assignments and assessments. Ensuring that the due dates are shared beforehand is vital to serve adult learners better. This allows the learners to plan to ensure they set aside time to read the required materials and to work on the assignment/assessment.
5. Eliminating 'late policies' that result in point deductions for late submissions. This can remove stress levels for adult learners who may need extra time due to personal or professional commitments.

CONCLUSION

Adult learning is fundamentally unique compared with children's learning styles and methods. Ensuring flexibility and empathy with adult learners will go a long way. Promoting flexible learning environments will allow adult learners to feel empowered, motivated, and determined to start an educational program and finish it. Flexible learning strategies can decrease barriers that may keep learners from furthering their education. Additionally, flexibility will ensure that adult learners are able to further their education, and potentially lead to chances of promotion or career changes. This can also assist with unemployment crises by offering flexible programs for adult learners. Education and higher income also have an impact on greater aspects of society, by improving socioeconomic status.

REFERENCES

Bellare, Y., Smith, A., Cochran, K., & Lopez, S. G. (2023). Motivations and barriers for adult learner achievement: Recommendations for institutions of higher education. *Adult Learning, 34*(1), 30–39. https://doi.org/10.1177/10451595211059574

Brown, E. A., Kinder, H., Stang, G. & Shumpert, W. (2023). Using adult learning characteristics and the humanities to teach undergraduate healthcare students about social determinants of health. *Humanities & Social Sciences communications, 10*(1), 114. https://doi.org/10.1057/s41599-023-01599-w

Midwestern higher education compact. (2021). *The digital divide among college students: Lessons learned from the COVID-19 emergency transition.* https://www.mhec.org/sites/default/files/resources/2021The_Digital_Divide_among_College_Students_1.pdf

Niksadat, N., Rakhshanderou, S., Negarandeh, R., Ramezankhani, A., Farahani, A. V. & Ghaffari, M. (2022). Concordance of the cardiovascular patient education with the principles of Andragogy model. *Archives of Public Health = Archives belges de sante publique, 80*(1), 4. https://doi.org/10.1186/s13690-021-00763-5

Penn State Outreach and Online Education. (2016, May). *Outreach and analytics reporting.* Adult Learner Profile.

ADDITIONAL READINGS

Ajani, O. A. (2023). Teaching professional development activities in Africa: Insights from South African high school teachers' experiences. *International Journal of Research in Business and Social Science.* https://www.researchgate.net/publication/376438346_Teacher_professional_development_activities_in_Africa_Insights_from_South_African_high_school_teachers'_experiences

Knowles, M. S., Holton, E. F. & Swanson, R. A. (2005). *The adult learner: The definitive classic in adult education and human resource development* (6th ed.). Elsevier.